Ju

MW00695655

Your _____, Vol IV

11 Inspiring Entrepreneurs Share Stories and Strategies on How to Jumpstart Many Areas of Your Life, Business, Health, and Prosperity

Compiled by Katrina Sawa

CEO & Founder of
www.JumpstartYourBizNow.com
and www.JumpstartPublishing.net

Jumpstart
PUBLISHING

Get to Know the 11 Inspiring Authors in this Book!

There's ONE page online where you can access all the authors' websites and special offers from this book to make it super easy for you to follow up and connect with them further.

Go to www.JumpstartBookAuthors.com right now before you forget.

Katrina Sawa, Speaker, Best-Selling Author, Award-Winning Business & Marketing Coach to Entrepreneurs Who Want More LOVE in Their Lives and MONEY in Their Businesses!

Published by K. Sawa Marketing International Inc. A.K.A. Jumpstart Publishing
P.O. Box 6, Roseville, CA 95661. (916) 872-4000
www.JumpstartPublishing.net

DISCLAIMER AND/OR LEGAL NOTICES
While all attempts have been made to verify information provided in this book and its ancillary materials, neither the authors nor publisher assume any responsibility for errors, inaccuracies, or omissions and are not responsible for any financial loss by customer in any manner. Any slights of people or organizations are unintentional. If advice concerning legal, financial, accounting, health or related matters is needed, the services of a qualified professional should be sought. This book and its associated ancillary materials, including verbal and written training, are not intended for use as a source of legal, financial or accounting advice.

EARNINGS & INCOME DISCLAIMER
With respect to the reliability, accuracy, timeliness, usefulness, adequacy, completeness, and/or suitability of information provided in this book, Katrina Sawa, K. Sawa Marketing International Inc., its partners, associates, affiliates, consultants, and/or presenters make no warranties, guarantees, representations, or claims of any kind. Readers' results will vary. This book and all products and services are for educational and informational purposes only. Katrina Sawa and/or K. Sawa Marketing International Inc. is not responsible for the success or failure of your business, personal, health or financial decisions relating to any information presented by Katrina Sawa, K. Sawa Marketing International Inc., or company products/services.

Any examples, stories, reference, or case studies are for illustrative purposes only and should not be interpreted as testimonies and/or examples of what readers and/or consumers can generally expect from the information.

ISBN: 978-1-7358666-2-8
PRINTED IN THE UNITED STATES OF AMERICA

Dedication

This book is dedicated to Entrepreneurs everywhere who have the desire and mission to make a bigger impact with those they serve.

Here's to creating and enjoying the business and life of your dreams!

Special thank you to my husband Jason and step-daughter Riley who support me 100% on all of my entrepreneurial endeavors. And thank you to all of the awesome jumpstart authors that have written their stories and strategies in this and previous books.

Praise for the *Jumpstart Your* _____ Books

These are my favorite books to read.

"This is the perfect time for this book to come out. I'm so glad I bought this! So many incredible stories of ways to jumpstart your business, your love life, your dreams, anything you can think of. These are my favorite books to read. I definitely recommend this book!" - Candi & Sean Douglas

Great read -- Short doses of inspiration

"This is a great book. Many tidbits of motivation. You can read any chapter and gain inspiration to take on the day's challenges. I love the stories and perspectives provided." - Karen T. Peak

Another great book by Katrina Sawa & Friends

"Katrina Sawa always brings her readers beneficial info for growing a business in the current marketplace." - PK Odle

Excellent Co-Authors with a variety of backgrounds

"Really great content, the authors here have a variety of backgrounds which is great for insight!" - Matt Brauning

A Great Source of Inspiration!

"Being an Entrepreneur is a really tough... but rewarding job! Sometimes you need a little extra encouragement to push you through the rough times. This is an incredible book, packed with all kinds of inspiring entrepreneur stories. I found nuggets of wisdom and inspiration all at the same time!" - Richard B. Greene

Katrina Sawa Never Disappoints

"Katrina Sawa never disappoints when she is delivering information to her audience of fans and she certainly delivers with her latest book. Thank you, Katrina, for gathering this group of experts to provide us with a great resource." - RL Escobar-Balcom

There is something for Everyone!

"Jumpstart Your _____ is filled with powerful stories and insightful takeaways that can help you grow your business and more importantly, enjoy your life. There is something for everyone! Bottom line - this book ROCKS!" - Craig Duswalt, Keynote Speaker, Author, Podcaster, and Creator of the brands RockStar Marketing and Rock Your Life.

So much great Inspiration!

"Hard to believe so much great information is available in ONE book. Whatever you dream... you can achieve! You are bound to find something impactful in this book!" - Marguerite Crespillo

TABLE OF CONTENTS

This book is divided first by topics relating to jumpstarting one's life and self, then by business-oriented chapters. Within each section, chapters are categorized alphabetically.

Jumpstart Your **Website**

Introduction

This book, *Jumpstart Your _____, Volume IV*, is for you if you need a jumpstart in any area of your life, career, business, mindset, health, relationships, prosperity, beliefs, and more!

This is the fourth book in the *Jumpstart Your _____* series, and we keep getting new, fresh topics, content, and authors! This volume has 10 new authors in addition to myself. We have a wide variety of chapters, with advice for the business owner, woman, professional, mom, online marketer, as well as the person who wants to improve his or her life, health, and even relationship with themselves and/or significant other. It's fun to see who comes through with each book, and what expertise they bring.

The authors with whom I have collaborated on this book are experts in their industries and in what they teach. Our goal is to provide a book that shows you how and why you should consider jumpstarting many of the areas covered within these chapters.

If you enjoy any one or more of the stories and chapters within this book, please reach out and contact the author(s). They want to know that their chapter encouraged you, inspired you, or motivated you in some way. They also want to know how they can help you. Each author has provided some kind of next step or free gift at the end of their chapter, to give you the opportunity to learn more. Don't stop with this book: please take the initiative and reach out for more information, more help, and more advice for whatever you might be trying to jumpstart in your life right now. Who knows: maybe after your initial read-through of this book, you will pick it up a couple years from now and decide to jumpstart something else.

This edition of *Jumpstart Your* _____ can help literally anyone, I believe. There are chapters you'll find immediately helpful, and some you may not need until years from now--but keep it handy just in case, because you never know!

Half of the chapters in this book will help you jumpstart an area of your personal life, and half of them are geared more towards helping business owners. Whether or not you have a business, one day you may! Order extra copies of these books for friends, family, or clients; they will appreciate your thoughtfulness.

What about you? Do you have an area of expertise about which you could write in one of our Jumpstart Your _____ books? One thing I know to be true is that most entrepreneurs really do need a book in this day and age. You need to be an author to really be seen as the expert in your industry, or even in the company for which you work. Writing a whole book by yourself is a lot of work, takes a lot of time, and sometimes costs a lot of money. Being an author in a compilation book like this one, however, is a lot less cumbersome, less stressful, and less costly. It's also helpful when somebody puts it all together for you, and you don't have to worry about all the details of editing, cover design, proofing, and publishing. (That's what we do here at Jumpstart Publishing.)

I've been in business since 2002. I've been an author in now 14 compilation books, plus two of my own full-length books. I have put together this opportunity to become a published author, with very little effort and work on your part--if you're interested. Contact me if you might be interested in being an author in the next *Jumpstart Your*_____ book, and share your story! Go to www.JumpstartPublishing.net for details.

And if you've ever thought about starting, growing, or marketing your own business, and/or becoming an author or speaker, please reach out to me; I'm extremely passionate about helping anybody build a profitable business doing what they love. - Katrina Sawa

Jumpstart Your Life/ Self Chapters

Jumpstart Your Assertiveness

How to Authentically Ask to Receive

By Katrina Sawa

Do you want more in your life? Out of your career? More revenues, clients, or a better lifestyle for you and your family?

If you do, then you might want to learn how to get more assertive.

Assertiveness is something that I discover is lacking in many small business owners and entrepreneurs. It's one of those things though that can make or break a business' success and it can either get you that promotion in your job, get you that partner you've been eyeballing and so much more.

If you really want what you say you want, then it's time to ASK for it!

Being assertive is simply asking for what you want more often than not. It's not sitting on the sidelines hoping the other person will make the move. Or hoping your boss or manager will acknowledge your performance enough to give you that raise or bonus.

Being assertive isn't being pushy or salesy either by the way. Being assertive is standing up for yourself, using your voice, and putting yourself out there in a way that people notice. Those are my definitions at least.

The official definition of Assertiveness according to Wikipedia is: *Assertiveness is the quality of being self-assured and confident without being aggressive. In the field of psychology and psychotherapy, it is a skill that can be learned and a mode of communication.*

So, why am I putting such emphasis on being more assertive whether it's in your life, relationships, career, or in your business?

It is because this is the foundation for sales and success in my mind. Those who assert themselves daily, get what they want and where they want to go faster. Those who reserve themselves and tend not to stand out or assert themselves generally take longer to get where they want to go, *IF they get there.*

Again, you can use this in your career or business for sure, I do. But you can also use it when dating; you can ask questions of your new date sooner than later to uncover whether they are a good match for you or not, or uncover the red flags sooner which is even more important!

You can use your assertiveness in your family life with your kids or significant others; if you want your kids to do chores or pick up their rooms, you need to ask them, right? If you want your significant other to help you around the house, you need to ask, right? Asking in a way that gets results is the key and, in each situation, with each person, that might warrant a different approach.

Especially in your business if you have one, I see entrepreneurs not being assertive enough in the sales process and then they end up making the amount of money that is below their expectations.

Being more assertive in your business is NOT pushy or uninviting. In fact, many people you talk to may want to use your services but because you aren't assertive enough in the follow-up process or with asking or inviting them to work with you or buy your products and programs, they feel underserved. You are NOT serving them by NOT being assertive. When they want what you've got and you don't make it easy for them to buy it, then YOU are the problem. You are self-sabotaging your own success... and theirs.

I've had to learn this skill myself over the last 50-something years. While I had a lot of "sales" and "marketing" training in my teens, 20's and even 30's, I had to practice asking more and asserting myself.

One year in my 20's, I even took a door-to-door sales job – WOW! That forced me to be more assertive!

We had to walk around neighborhoods and even into commercial areas just knocking on doors, asking people if they wanted what we were selling. It was very uncomfortable for the whole nine months I did this, but looking back on it, that was the best job I'd ever had to really teach me to be more assertive. This is because I had doors slammed in my face, people yelling at me and really harsh weather conditions at times also.

Now, as a business coach and entrepreneur, I always say; "I can take a NO, like nobody's business!"

Being able to take rejection relatively easy as a business owner or in dating, is a key skill you want to learn. That comes with being more assertive but know, most of the time, it's NOT personal.

When someone says "no" to you for whatever reason, there are three ways to look at it.

1. If they *really* mean no and there isn't just an excuse around it, then that's a blessing really because you can move on. I say "NEXT!" when that happens and don't let it bother me.

2. Many times, though, especially in business, they just mean *not right now* when they say "no".

3. A "no" can also mean that they don't have enough information yet to say "yes" and it's your job to show the value or give them more information, especially in business situations.

One of the main skills to master when you are in sales or when you run your own business is closing, conversion, enrolling, and holding effective sales conversations. You don't become very successful or profitable unless you learn how to sell well.

That doesn't mean you have to be salesy, annoying, sleazy, or pushy, however. It's a skill amongst many other skills you need to master. You just have to find the way that works for you, your style, your words, and your personality.

I consider myself a consultative salesperson. That means I ask a lot of questions, analyze situations, find out what people want, need or desire during the sales process. I make them feel special, heard and that I get them. I do that all because I care of course, after all, selling is serving.

Asking questions is the easiest way to be more assertive in fact. Just be curious. Be genuinely interested and curious with people; they'll like you more for it and you'll learn more information in the process.

When you're not assertive in your business, or you stay quiet and don't ask questions or ask for someone to take the next step to work with you or buy your products, then you don't make money. Yeah, you might get lucky and have a few prospects ask YOU how they can buy from you but that's pretty rare. Being unable to speak up typically means you aren't confident enough about what value you or your products bring.

And if you don't know your value or your worth, then you'll settle for less and that's no way to live. Life is too short.

Being unable to speak up at work or in a job can have long-lasting negative consequences. It can lead to stress, burnout, or render you almost invisible in a setting where promotions and raises depend on visibility.

When you're assertive, you ask for what you need, you talk openly about what you want, and you recognize when someone is taking advantage of you. You can approach the things you do with confidence and make a direct impact on your environment. But this does not come easily for everyone.

There are two important components to becoming more assertive:

1. Learning to treat yourself with respect
2. Building communication skills

If you don't respect yourself, others are less likely to respect you. That includes setting boundaries for yourself and situations you incur regularly. Taking on extra projects despite missing important family events, or continuing to answer work emails from your bed despite the interference with a proper night's rest—burnout is made of these ingredients. Think about what you can realistically expect of yourself and respect your limitations.

Learn the difference between being assertive and aggressive. Many people quiet their voices because they have come to believe that speaking up is the same as being bossy, pushy, or disrespectful of other people. Being assertive does not have to be any of those things; it only means you value your own thoughts, feelings, and voice as well as those of others.

You can continue to be a kind, likable person while communicating directly. Assertive communication doesn't look to bulldoze over other people (that would be aggressive communication). Saying, "I disagree with that" is assertive and honest, and it opens up further conversation. "What kind of stupid idea is that?" is aggressive and minimizing, and it shuts down conversation.

The more you learn and grow, the more connected you can feel to your skills and your knowledge. The more you know yourself, your value, and the things you can offer to the world around you, the more confident you will get. The more confident you get, the more clients and CASH you will attract!

Have patience with yourself as you make these changes. You may stumble through difficult conversations or lose your nerve at the last moment. That's OK—just be you. Be your amazing self and be open to building more great relationships. The more assertive you are in all areas of your life, the more you'll enjoy a life you love - I'm confident.

Sign up here for a complimentary consult around becoming more assertive, or anything and everything else involved with growing your small business: www.AskKat.biz

You can also download and access a bunch of free trainings to help you start-up, grow, monetize, and maximize your business on my website at www.JumpstartYourBizNow.com/freetrainings.

Here's to stretching yourself to get what you want!

About the Author

Katrina Sawa

The JumpStart Your Biz Coach, Katrina Sawa, is the creator of the JumpStart Your Marketing & Sales Systems, and an Int'l Best-Selling author including *Love Yourself Successful* and *Jumpstart Your New Business Now*. She is the CEO of JumpstartYourBizNow.com and JumpstartPublishing.net. Katrina's no-nonsense approach develops consistently profitable businesses implementing proven marketing and business strategies. She's been featured on the Oprah and Friends XMRadioNetwork, ABC, TheCW and dozens of influential podcasts.

Jumpstart Your Conflict Resolution

2 Keys to Resolve Any Dispute

By Dr. Grace Gwitira

In a world where diversity includes that of race, background, religion, disability, age, gender, personalities, and perspectives, **conflict is inevitable**.

Conflict can lead to:

- Increased stress levels

- Reduced morale, motivation, and productivity

- Loss of employment, promotion, or salary raises

- Miscommunication, misunderstandings, and broken relationships

- Diminished confidence and self-esteem

- Fear and inability to stand in your power

- Social disharmony and violence

There isn't anyone I know who doesn't experience conflict in one way or another. Whether it's in your personal life, your professional life or within yourself, you must find ways to resolve disputes so you can stand your ground and plead your case in a logical, composed manner that yields positive results.

In the last 20 years, I've dealt with several conflict situations in my life and helped others resolve hundreds of disputes in their personal and professional lives resulting in positive outcomes. I help clients navigate through conflict in my emotional intelligence training and coaching practice. Based on my decades of experience, I realize that most people don't know how to handle conflict for the good of all. During the conflict, their negative emotions drive their actions, resulting in worsening the situation and leaving the issue unresolved. Unresolved conflict can create damage which is sometimes difficult to repair as negative feelings fester.

What conflict situation have you experienced that you or someone else did not handle well? How do you feel about it? How you handle conflict determines whether the outcome is *for bitter* or for better.

By Dr. Grace Gwitira

"If we manage conflict constructively,
we harness its energy for creativity and development."
– Kenneth Kaye

The 2 Keys you need to unlock and harness your power and resolve any dispute constructively lie in the two areas of emotional intelligence: **intra**personal intelligence and **inter**personal intelligence.

Intrapersonal Intelligence

Intrapersonal intelligence or self-awareness involves knowing yourself—being aware of your thoughts, feelings, tempers, attitudes, strengths, weaknesses, limitations, desires, and motivations. It enables you to know what areas you need to develop, and which areas are serving you well. It also allows you to manage your emotions more effectively leading you to respond to others in more constructive ways. For example, if you are unpleasant to be around when you don't get enough sleep, self-awareness would drive you to go to bed on time so that you can be pleasant and be at your best the next day.

Another example where self-awareness plays a role is if you may have or are experiencing personal conflict or internal conflict as you battle between the decision to leave a secure job you've hated and had for years and seeking another or starting your own business. Perhaps you have reached a glass ceiling and are thus restricted from bringing about the influence and impact you desire in the world. While you know that to fully become who God created you to be and

17

live your purpose, it is necessary to take that one step, your mind and your heart are in contention with each other, leaving you paralyzed to act. Self-awareness will give you the motivation to take the less comfortable step that will propel you toward your purpose.

Personal conflict is important to address because of its negative impact on your wellbeing as well as its undesirable effect on how you show up to people in your personal and professional life. It can even be the precursor for some of the conflict occurrences in your life. When you have a high level of intrapersonal intelligence, you can, when provoked, stop, think, and then respond, versus just randomly reacting to every negative stimulus. Self-awareness arms you with the tools needed to resolve conflict within yourself and conflict with others, which is an aspect of interpersonal intelligence.

Interpersonal Intelligence

Interpersonal Intelligence includes the ability to manage the emotions of others. It involves social awareness and using empathy to understand how others feel and give appropriate responses. With interpersonal skills, you can communicate, connect, and collaborate better. These skills are important for conflict resolution.

Just as conflict exists in your personal life, it also exists in your professional life. When people from diverse backgrounds, interests and thinking exist in the same space, there will be conflict. The presence of conflict is not necessarily a bad thing. If the parties involved commit to finding an amicable solution, the results can be beneficial to those involved and to the organization.

I used to manage a team of permit specialists whose responsibilities included processing email requests from a single email queue and responding to the sender appropriately. Some team members complained that they handled more emails than others. Those who were accused of not pulling their weight fought back, citing that they worked on other projects and that they were doing their part in handling the email queue. The dispute was resolved by installing an email distribution program that automatically distributed emails equitably among the specialists. The program tracked the time each email was handled, who handled it, and how many emails each person handled within a given time. This enabled proper tracking, improved efficiencies, and resolved the conflict. Had the conflict not occurred, the program might not have been implemented.

Conflict is good when it drives those involved to adopt a CIA (Communication, Innovation, and Acceptance) Culture. If you want to be the leader, expert, entrepreneur, or influencer who effectively navigates through conflict and brings out the best in people, then you must harness your interpersonal intelligence and take the lead in creating a CIA Culture.

A. Communication

To be great at conflict resolution, you must create a culture of open and honest communication.

When two parties are involved in a dispute, communication is stifled. The two may not have anything pleasant to say to each other and therefore choose to give each other the silent treatment.

For example, I heard a story about a couple giving each other the silent treatment following a contentious encounter. The husband, maintaining his stance not to speak to his wife, left a note asking her to wake him up at 6:00 am the next morning. The next morning at 6:00 am, the wife left a note for her sleeping husband saying, "it's time to wake up." He ended up being late for his engagement and could not blame the wife who had silently played her part.

In a professional team environment, failing to communicate effectively can hinder the team from making progress. So, when team members are in conflict, it is necessary for you, as the leader, or business owner to intervene and facilitate communication. You can help by allowing each person to voice their side of the story while you remain neutral. Begin by setting the ground rules for how the interaction will be conducted.

For example, No yelling, pointing fingers, or attacking the other person personally. Using phrases like "when you did _____ I felt _____" can help by removing accusatory language from the dialogue. Statements like, "what I hear you saying is_____" are helpful because oftentimes, conflict arises from pre-conceived notions, wrong assumptions, and misunderstandings.

B. Innovation

Innovation can be birthed from conflict when the parties involved create a solution outside of themselves.

For example, two employees were arguing about the best application to use for a project that requires creating tables. Janelle believed that using Microsoft Word was the best because she had used it before in her university assignments and created beautiful tables. Toniel believed using Microsoft Excel was easier because that's what he usually uses when doing any work that requires tables. The two argued about which application to use and finally, they decided to use Microsoft Access, citing that the application will enable them to be able to run queries and reports which will, in the long run, make it easier for them.

Thus, the conflict was resolved by collaborating on what is best for the project versus what is individually easier, resulting in finding a new way that is acceptable to both -- creating an opportunity for innovation.

C. Acceptance

Acceptance stems from the ability to recognize that people are different. We live in an environment where diversity exists. When you look at a situation, you are looking at it from a certain perspective, predicated by your background, upbringing, and knowledge.

Thus, to implement a culture of acceptance:

1. Allow others to see the situation from their perspective.
2. Seek first to understand before jumping to conclusions about the intentions or abilities of others.
3. Listen intently and actively, without interrupting.
4. Exercise empathy -- What would life be like if you were that person in that situation?
5. Find ways to be supportive while finding a collaborative solution

You can develop your ability to resolve conflict, improve relationships, and inspire the best in others by developing your intrapersonal intelligence and interpersonal intelligence, both components of emotional intelligence.

I invite you to explore deeper with me. I have free gifts especially created for you on my website. You will receive:

1. Report: How to Avoid Self-Sabotaging Your Own Success
2. Training: Self-Regulation is Your Secret Superpower to Success

3. A Complimentary Consultation with me valued at $360. How can I be of service to you?

Get your free gifts now at
   www.DrGraceGwitira.com/jumpstart

Let's get those conflicts resolved!!

About the Author

Dr. Grace Gwitira

Dr. Grace Gwitira is an award-winning author, speaker, trainer, and certified emotional intelligence coach. With a Doctor of Management in Organizational Leadership degree, she helps her clients to overcome stress, overwhelm, anxiety, anger; increase motivation; develop conflict resolution skills, and have productive relationships so that they can inspire others to action and make more money while doing what they love. She is the Founder and CEO of Transformation Oasis.

Jumpstart Your Connection

4 Keys to More Connection with Yourself and Others

By Agnes Loughlin

You don't have to be alone to feel lonely. Whether you think you need more joy and connection or not, loneliness is a top-of-mind issue for many people right now.

According to Signa Global Health, prior to COVID, 61% of people in the U.S. reported feeling lonely sometimes or all the time. AARP reports that since COVID, 66-86% of people in the U.S. report feeling lonely. According to Dr. Lissa Rankin, loneliness is the number one factor in the cause of disease including heart disease, depression, and cognitive health.

"Relationships are assignments made by God; people are drawn together who represent a maximal opportunity for soul growth... The miracle is simply a shift in perception, a change that occurs inside ourselves." - Marianne Williamson

When we struggle with loneliness, we may give up on finding connected relationships, or we may even find acceptance and acknowledgement in the most unusual of circumstances. This is my story.

On a cold day in January, about two weeks before my 8th birthday, I went to live with my two siblings in Guardian Angel Orphanage in Peoria, Illinois. My mom felt stressed at the thought of raising three young children alone while working a full-time job. The orphanage, run by nuns, was a big sprawling building with separate sections for boys and girls. My sister 6 1/2 years old and I were in the girl's section. My 3 1/2year old brother went to the nursery.

Life was regimented. I was assigned two dresses to wear. I slept in a bed in a big dormitory on the third floor. There was a school across from the main building also run by the nuns. Each child was assigned housekeeping chores to help keep everything running smoothly: setting the tables for eating, doing dishes, scrubbing floors, etc. On arising at 6:30 am, we immediately made our beds and proceeded to go to the chapel on the floor below for morning mass.

My lonely life became even lonelier. Despite being surrounded by many children, I felt little connection or desire to play. Some of the children were in emotional turmoil, that I had little understanding of. I found solace though, in a library of books. Fairy tales caught my attention. Here was a magical way to connect to a fantasy reality of beautiful young girls, with challenges and opportunities. I was enchanted. Life was full of adventures that always ended happily.

I met my husband in my freshman year of college. We connected over a book, *A Many Splendored Thing* by Han Suyin. He said the writer reminded him of me. We married 3 years later. Life with a functional alcoholic husband was also lonely. I could have become the victim of this situation. However, I covered this loneliness in busyness with little awareness that attracting friendship, required me to step out of myself and be a friend.

I became a nurse at the age of 50 after working in 2 previous roles in health care. Drawing me out of my shell was a gradual process. I think it accelerated when I joined some nurses in Nikken, selling wellness products. I was drawn out of my comfort zone as I forced myself to talk to people. Although I did not feel confident in doing so, I was busy and more engaged. Perhaps, it was the Universe saying: "I have a better plan for you."

One day, my loneliness took a big turn. A physician whom I had met 4 months earlier, asked me to come to Michigan to pick her up and take her to Chicago to get her car which had needed some repair work. As we drove back to Chicago, she started telling me about herself in a very engaging way. She felt like a victim in her life.

Sharon was extremely intelligent and very believable and engaging in some ways. I lent an ear and energy of acceptance. The energy of acceptance and acknowledgment was what we both deeply wanted.

After 19 days, I was exasperated about the close living arrangements and asked Sharon to leave.

Upon realizing that she was gone, I felt distraught. I had in some ways felt a deep connection to someone who listened intently to what I would say; someone who would enter the kitchen and cook and converse with me. On some levels, I felt a sense of connection that had been missing. I felt heard.

I asked a friend for advice. Phil listened and recommended a book: *Power versus Force* by David R Hawkins. I purchased the book right away and started reading. I felt divinely guided and my life changed immediately. I felt a sense of connection to myself that was different. I said, love was the only thing that mattered. I said I was going to live in a higher level of awareness; I was going to create this.

I continued my education in several healing modalities which helped me feel a much deeper sense of connection to myself. I was the one who really changed. My husband even changed and abruptly stopped drinking 6 1/2 years later.

My new sense of joy and connection has filled me with a desire to empower others to create connection and self-love. This is done through releasing emotional baggage, limiting beliefs, meditations, retreats. You can create that inner miracle for yourself through an inner change in perception.

In my current coaching and healing business, I share some powerful ways people can achieve more connection as well as more joy in their lives; and I want to share a few tips with you here.

4 Keys to More Connection

1. Become aware of the symptoms and causes of loneliness.

Clues to loneliness include anxiety, busyness, procrastination, and health challenges. Depression is more common in women.

I recommend that we become aware that connection and love are a state of being and wholeness, not a passing feeling. Read some books on how to build more love and connection with yourself. Email me and I will share a list of books. I also recommend Louise Hay's mirror strategy. Whenever you look in a mirror, smile and say: "I love myself." Say it multiple times a day.

2. Release your limiting beliefs about your self-worth

What are your daily thoughts predominantly about? The subconscious mind is said to control 88% of the operating system of our conscious mind. These beliefs are meant to protect us and keep us the same. They often prevent us from making changes to our lives that would empower us.

How would a person know if she has a limiting belief? Guess what! We all have them! Most of the beliefs are from our ancestors. I find them through muscle testing. They are simple to release with the support of a healer/coach. I recommend Theta Healing which is similar to hypnosis but much more.

Most people think they already do love themselves. However, this is their conscious mind speaking. Limiting beliefs affect relationships, money, body image, and all areas of life. Release some limiting beliefs today and become a new you!

3. Create your life with tools and a map

Most have a fuzzy vision and map to create their life. Without changing oneself, a person will be plagued by chronic dissatisfaction or a superficial vision of the possibilities. As long as a person looks to other people to feel accepted and connected, she will keep searching.

A map or blueprint is about creating your life in all 4 quadrants or relationships: mind, body/health, people/relationships, and external creations including money and career endeavors. Our joy and connection are found in our creativity and living in the present. This is a process and is possible. I use and love the Higher Brain Living map and creation process.

4. Jumpstart your Relationships

Relationships are the lynchpin of life. To create more fulfilling relationships, focus on creating face-to-face meaningful conversations. Converse with a spouse or special friend. Converse with a stranger—yes, a stranger is just a friend whom you have not met or connected with.

I recommend connecting with a variety of people to satisfy a variety of needs and desires. Do not expect only one person to satisfy all your needs—this is giving your power away. Connect with those who give you a sense of being fully alive.

My new sense of joy and connection has filled me with a desire to empower you to create more connection and self-love. This is done through releasing emotional baggage, limiting beliefs, meditations, and retreats. You can create that inner miracle for yourself through an inner change in perception.

Hopefully, I've inspired you to think about your own life and the connections you create. My goal is to show you how to create more self-love, worthiness and empower your creativity. Suffering is a choice. **I have created a few free gifts for you on my website at www.MiraclesInWellness.com/jumpstart. You can get access to the following:**

- Download my complimentary guide: "Ten Ways to Have More Joy and Connection Today"

- Experience a short meditation: "Expand the Love in Your Life"

- Plus get an opportunity to have a call with me so we can uncover together what's really going on.

Here's to more connection, love and joy in your life!

About the Author
Agnes Loughlin

Agnes founded Miracles in Wellness in 2011. She has a background as a nurse, nurse practitioner, facilitates retreats and meditations. She is certified in The Emotion Code, Parasite Healing, Theta Healing, Higher Brain Living®, Potentiate Your DNA®, and a life coach. She believes that we are spiritual beings living a human experience. We heal on many levels. Agnes empowers her clients to expand in self-love and create aliveness in all their relationships.

Jumpstart Your Hormones

3 Areas to Giving You Your Life Back

By Dr. Erin Foley DC, CFMP

As a Functional Medicine nutrition and hormone specialist, I see women struggling with their health and hormones every day, and many who have no idea that what they're struggling with actually has to do with their hormones and it's fixable. They don't know what they don't know. I hope that you will identify a few areas in this chapter that can give you a new awareness to what's going on with your body.

As women, we have ages and stages of life. And each one can be vibrant, healthy and enjoyable. You have your childbearing years in your 30's and 40's, peri-menopause in your 40's, and menopause in your 50s. These stages can overlap and occur at different times for different women, and at each stage, your female hormones do different things.

First off, let me explain about your "female hormones", these are not what I want to share in this chapter, but you need to know the difference. Your "female hormones" are your estrogen, progesterone and also include testosterone. This is your fertility, your menstrual cycle, and the transition into peri-menopause and menopause, and most women think about these hormones first.

But the hormones I want to talk about and help you with are:

- Your **stress hormones**, adrenals and cortisol, which are your "fight or flight" hormones. These hormones help you manage stress, and if out of balance, can cause belly fat gain, weight gain, low energy, low mood and sleeping difficulty.

- You also have your **blood sugar hormones** which include insulin. These hormones are key to having a healthy weight, energy, sleep and mood. You need to make sure you balance your blood sugar and insulin, otherwise, they can cause pre-diabetes and diabetes. This can be controlled with what you eat.

- And last but not least, you have your **thyroid hormone** that controls your metabolism.

By Dr. Erin Foley DC, CFMP

These three hormones are all connected to your female hormones, and everything works together.

The struggle is real. The struggle with weight, sleep, energy, mood, PMS, hot flashes, gut health and so much more, is one of the reasons I do what I do.

I am privileged to have had a long career in natural health care as a chiropractor and acupuncturist. I have always been passionate about helping people with their health. Now I exclusively help women with functional medicine, nutrition, lifestyle and gut health issues in my Vibrant Healthy Woman Programs.

In 2003, I was diagnosed with Hashimoto's, which is an autoimmune low thyroid disease. I had all the symptoms, the weight gain, the fatigue, the sleep issues and female hormones issues. I sought out functional medicine practitioners to help me with my own healing journey.

The beauty of functional medicine is that it's a natural health care and it helps you get to the root cause of health and hormone issues. Nutrition, lifestyle, stress reduction, hormone testing, supplements and gut health are all the key things you want to pay attention to.

The most important thing for you to know is that no matter where you are with your health and hormones, and no matter what age you are, you can heal. You can influence your health and hormones with your nutrition, lifestyle, supplements and gut health. What you do every day matters!

Here are the 3 essential areas to look at regarding your hormones and what you can do about them.

1. Healthy Nutrition Creates Healthy Hormones

What you eat every day can heal or hinder your hormones. When you eat, your food contains protein, fats and carbohydrates, and it's the carbohydrates that will affect your blood sugar the most. If you eat too much sugar or too many refined carbs, this can raise your blood sugar and your insulin hormone must come to the rescue to balance it. However, your insulin sensitivity mechanism can break down after years of too much sugar and too many carbs.

It doesn't help that there is so much confusion about what to eat.

To bring your blood sugar into balance, do these things:

Use a tracking App to find out how many carbs, proteins and fats you are eating per day. Then look at what you are eating. Are you eating packaged, processed, sugary foods? Soda or energy drinks? Fast food or junk food? Do you order take-out a lot?

The foods that you want to eat are whole foods such as animal proteins, healthy fats (like real butter, coconut and olive oils, avocados, nuts), vegetables, and fruits as the core of your plate. There are so many good healthy foods to eat and healthy meal delivery services.

What about pasta, bread, rice, cereal, and beans? These foods are high in carbohydrates and can cause a blood sugar rollercoaster. It is really individual on how you handle these, but most women feel more energy, sleep better and lose weight when they minimally include those foods.

2. Your Lifestyle and Breaking the Cycle of Stress

I know you know what stress is, but it can also be vague. Stress comes from your lifestyle and can unbalance ALL your hormones. This is not something to ignore or put off acting on.

Stress in your life can show up as being too busy or overwhelmed, doing it all and not making yourself a priority. This can be from relationships, family, spouse, job or business, money, caregiving, physical injury and so much more.

Are you trying to do it all, all the time? Are you taking care of everyone but you?

Something will have to give, and usually, it will be you and your hormones.

Your stress hormones are your "fight or flight" hormones and are an ancestral survival mechanism meant to put your body into fast action to run, fight, freeze or hide in response to a threat.

But now, the common thing for women is to be activating your stress hormones daily in response to your everyday life. This can cause your main adrenal hormones, cortisol, to become unbalanced and be high or low. This can cause weight gain and belly fat, tiredness and extreme fatigue, inability to sleep, low mood, and it can contribute to PMS or hot flashes.

To Break the Cycle of Stress, do these things:

Sit with yourself and be honest. What is your stress and lifestyle like? What do you need to change? What would you like your life and health to look like?

What are some ways you can let go of things, hire or enlist family help around your house, an assistant in your business perhaps, and/or hire help to improve your health?

What is your Self-Care like? What can you add in that will nurture and nourish you?

Self-care comes in many flavors, and that can be an activity such as a massage, pedicure, creating art or being with friends. It can also be downtime, a nap, a hot bath, reading, writing or watching a movie. There are so many ways to do it, you need to find your self-care style, and then schedule it in!

Self-care is also about having boundaries and learning to say "No". Stop overcommitting and care for yourself first!

The next part of breaking the cycle of stress is keeping your blood sugar balanced. If you are eating too many carbs and sugars for your body, you can start having cravings and stress eating. And, if you are stress eating the not-so-healthy foods, this will put you on the blood sugar rollercoaster and keep the stress cycle going.

Getting your hormones tested is a great first step. Find out what is going on with your body now!

It's all about bringing balance to your adrenal and cortisol hormones, calming your fight or flight hormones down, and having stable blood sugar. This will allow you to have good sleep, good energy, a good stable mood, and motivation to make healthy choices and be at a healthy weight.

All these things are possible!

3. Evaluate your Hormones

Hormone Testing and evaluation is a tool that can really help you if you are having issues with energy, sleep, weight, mood, or even with hot flashes and PMS. I use hormone testing, nutrition and lifestyle assessment tools with clients. This can show exactly where you are now, at your age and give you a baseline.

Together, we can create a program for you to move forward with confidence to vibrant health.

I see so many women who are "falling through the cracks" of modern medicine. Women tell me they are being told by their doctors that they are "too young" or "too old" to be tested or evaluated. You can get testing done by someone like me or a functional medicine doctor in your area. I truly believe, and have seen with my own body, and my patients and clients, that hormones and aging do not have to be hard!

My message to you is one of HOPE. You can be vibrant and healthy at ANY age, you just need to know what is going on.

If you would like to thrive with your hormones and health and want to know how you can do it naturally, then, **I put together a few resources for you on my website. Go to www.JumpstartYourHormones.com** and you'll get access to the following:

- A Free Health and Hormone Discovery Call with me

- A Free Guide: "5 Steps for Women to have more Energy over 40"

- Free Masterclass series on "Hormones and Pleasure" and "The Magic of Menopause"

I look forward to helping you thrive with your health and hormones, not just surviving!

About the Author

Dr. Erin Foley, DC, CFMP

Dr. Erin Foley is a Functional Medicine Practitioner and Chiropractor with Vibrant Healthy Woman Programs. She helps women balance their hormones naturally, helping with energy, sleep, weight, metabolism, mood, mental clarity, gut, digestion, hormones, hot flashes, PMS, and helping you create vibrant health. She works with women with hormone testing programs, online group coaching, online private coaching programs, online courses, and natural solutions for gut health and mental wellness.

Jumpstart Your Limitless Potential

5 Essential Steps to Convert your Dreams into Reality

By Lynn Swearingen

Potential is a word we are all familiar with. We think we know what it means, but do we really? When I decided to write about potential, I looked up the definition.

POTENTIAL = latent qualities or abilities that may be developed and lead to future success or usefulness.
But notice: *Latent defined as "a quality or state existing but not yet developed or manifest; hidden or concealed."*

Where is it "hidden or concealed"? Your subconscious mind is a massive warehouse of potential. It is filled with resources, tools, capabilities, characteristics, intelligence, memory, life experiences and gifts that are yours and yours alone. Most people never tap into their unlimited resources. The steps outlined in this chapter will help you unleash your inner brilliance and live the life you've only dared to dream.

Are you tired of spinning your wheels and feeling lost, stuck, doubtful, worried? Do you feel like you just can't get started or that your dream is too big? You may have a brilliant plan, a strategy for success, and a burning passion to get out there and just do it. If you feel out of your depth – then this information is exactly for you.

If you could wave a magic wand and have anything you want … what would that be? No one is given a passion or a calling without the means to make it happen.
Implementing these steps will take you on an amazing journey of self-discovery you will highly value as you live and grow into your dreams.

5 Essential Steps to Convert your Dreams into Reality

Step 1: Change Your Story

Your story and your thoughts have power beyond your imagination. The story you tell yourself is what you become; it is who you are. If you don't learn to control your thoughts, your thoughts will control you. Your thoughts will lift you up and make you an unstoppable force of nature, OR … they will crush you.

You are in control. You have the capacity to examine your thoughts and emotions and respond accordingly in a positive, rational way. You can choose what you want and what you don't want in your life. And *failure to make a choice is also a choice.* You can reframe your perception of reality. You can choose what version of yourself you will be in this present moment.

Every thought simultaneously connects to an emotional response and a physical response, leading you to a corresponding behavior or outcome.

What if you have a big presentation at work and you notice your harsh inner critic barging in with negative, overly critical thoughts, but this time you respond differently. You say 'no' to that story and instead, you say:

I am intelligent, competent, and strong. I am an engaging speaker. I am a rock star and I rock this talk!

Your subconscious believes that what you tell it is true. Now you're ready to roll, operating on all cylinders, at optimal capacity. You feel a dynamic flow of resources, intelligence, tools, and expertise. You are a success before you even step out!

What are your stories? You have many. You have stories about your family ... your marriage or romantic relationships, or lack of ... your children ... your career ...

your opportunities in life, and more. What is your story about your POTENTIAL?

Step 2: Change Your State

Success is a State of Mind. Only YOU have the power to change your inner state. Only YOU can step up your inner game.

You probably have noticed that you can make yourself happy or sad, hot or cold, healthy or sick, just by your thoughts and imagination. You can ramp up to a state of fear. But you can learn to control your inner state and change your inner game.

Regardless of your specific set of obstacles and challenges, your life experiences have given you unique perspectives, which establish your position to contribute to the world in very personal, insightful ways.

Regardless of genetics, environment, nurture, or nature, if you've been given a dream, you've been given the resources to fulfill that dream.

Students who major in Communications quickly learn the importance of connection through stories and emotion. It isn't enough to lay out the facts. We GET it when we hear a story that moves us, and when we FEEL what's being said and CONNECT with it at a deep inner level. Then we remember. We feel compelled to act. Otherwise, it's just another boring set of facts soon forgotten.

Are you telling yourself a new story, but it isn't landing?
To change your state, it is imperative to connect with your new story emotionally and physically.

What happens when you add an emotional reward to a positive statement – *and I feel?*

What if you physically respond in support of that emotion – *raise a fist, or jump in the air?*

Create a state of certainty. Don't just say words. Go ALL IN with your emotions and physical body. Say YES to change. Shout YES to the world. Put your body into it. With that state of certainty, sound out your new story with emotional conviction, with utter self-belief, physically and emotionally connecting to what you say. Feel your inner state rise, your frequency, rising ever higher!

Nothing is more powerful than an "I am" statement: I am ... I do ... I go ... simultaneously connecting emotionally and physically. Speak to yourself in the present tense. It's OK to 'fake it 'til you make it' because you are telling your subconscious THIS is who I am NOW. People will respond to you differently.

You will be inspired, grounded in your authentic power, and will rock your world!

Step 3: Get Your Subconscious on the Same Page

You have a massive store of gifts, resources, tools, intelligence, and talents. You have important dreams and goals. The world needs you to be generous with your gifts, to unleash your inner brilliance and be your best self. We are all connected in magical, mysterious ways, and all of us are depending on you to fulfil your potential.

Do you feel "the harder I try, the harder it gets?" Like having a fight with yourself? That's because you are. The "fight with yourself" occurs when you decide in your conscious mind, but your subconscious says "no." Your subconscious cannot tell the difference between what you imagine and what is real. So, what may *feel* like an inner saboteur is your subconscious trying to help, as it responds to a misleading story you just told it.

Make it a constant practice to imagine your success, your joy, your accomplishments. You are the boss of your imagination. If you can imagine it all going wrong, you can imagine it all going right. Vividly imagine your storybook ending. See yourself flowing towards your goals in the future you create. Let your inner superhero fly.

Step 4: The Care and Feeding of your Beautiful Subconscious Mind

Most likely, you know the importance of eating proper foods to serve your nutritional needs. You understand the importance of regular exercise and the need for stimulating mental activity for brain health. You probably pay attention to your spiritual needs and practices. We've heard time and again to tend to our body, mind and spirit.

Would it ever occur to you to think, *"I ate three well-balanced meals today, so I don't need to eat for the rest of the week?"* Of course not, that would be silly. But when was the last time you considered what you are feeding your subconscious mind?

If you are not continually programming your subconscious with what you need, want and desire, your life will quickly go off track. It may happen gradually or suddenly. You won't even know what happened until it's too late, because you weren't paying attention!

Step 5: Rinse and Repeat

So now you know the simple formula.
Change your STORY, change your LIFE. Examine your thoughts and emotions. Change what doesn't serve you.
Change your STATE. Maximize your Inner Game by supporting your new story with strong emotional and physical connections.
IMAGINE things going well.

Tend to the CARE and FEEDING of your subconscious mind. Program your subconscious with intention and purpose. Feed it what it needs to unleash your full potential.

And everything goes so well ... for this week and the next. Perhaps for a month ... a year ... or longer. And then life smacks you in the face and you have a knee-jerk reaction. You suddenly revert to old worry, doubt, and fear.

Turn insight into action. You learned the power of your mind and your power to change thoughts and emotions. You learned how to change your story and your state moving forward with confidence and certainty. So now, it's up to you.

I invite you to go to my website at https://lynnswearingen.kartra.com/page/jumpstart to get access to 3 free gifts to Jumpstart Your Limitless Potential:

- My Free eBook "5 Essential Steps to Love Your Life Again"

- A full hypnosis session to "Activate Your Inner Power"

- A free consultation to activate permanent, transformative change.

If you are serious about taking your life back, go get these free resources and start implementing these five easy steps today.

As you implement these steps, you will move fluidly and confidently toward your goals, self-correcting before going off course – resilient, adaptive, and flexible – unstoppable.

About the Author

Lynn C. Swearingen, CH, CI

Lynn is a Neuro-Linguistic Hypnotist, a Certified HypnoCoach® and Owner of Bay Area Hypnotherapy™. She is here to guide you to unleash your inner brilliance and limitless potential. An NGH Certified Instructor, Lynn is helping to mold the next wave of modern, science-based, transformative hypnotists.

Jumpstart Your Love Relationships

8 Lessons Learned to Creating Win-Win Relationships

By Katrina Sawa

Do you know what will ultimately change the world? One thing... love.

When more people love more and are IN love more, the world can finally be a place with more harmony, respect and happiness. Unfortunately, the people who really need to hear this message may not read it. But if you're reading it, you can still create that ripple effect into the world with the love you have and give.

Let's talk about your relationships. The relationships with yourself, your significant other if you have one (or multiple), your children if you have them, your parents if they are still living, other close family and friends and then the relationships with everyone else including your clients, employees, and business connections.

These are the relationships that make up your life. And whether or not your life goes smoothly, is in harmony, balance and that you're completely happy majority of the time or not depends on those relationships.

Therefore, it would make sense that you focus quite a bit of your energy on building up all of those relationships to be healthy, loving, respectful, supportive and strong.

So, how do we do that? Well, I'll share a few things I've learned over the last 40-50 years or so that work for me. Now, I'm not a psychiatrist, psychologist, therapist or even a relationship coach but I have been working with business owners for over 20 years. And business owners encounter all of the blocks anyone would have with themselves and others and those relationships often hold them back from doing the necessary things in their businesses to make more money if they're not going well. Therefore, I tend to talk a lot with clients about what I call the "love" side of their life... that's anything personal basically.

For example, I have two very good clients both going through nasty divorces this year. They are often distraught, overwhelmed, depressed, angry and just plain exhausted with the amount of energy they are having to expend finalizing all of that much less doing everything they need to do to keep their business not just afloat, but thriving. In fact, one of them reported to me just this week that she's made it over six figures this year already and it was only October! That's because she's determined, she keeps going, she has support like me but she's also hired an assistant and a couple of employees knowing she just couldn't manage it all by herself.

I have a client who last year left her big corporate job to finally live the life she'd always dreamed of with her own business, yes, but most of all, she and her newer husband wanted to move to a more rural area, get some dogs and focus more on their health and living their life, rather than working all the time. She's doing all of that now and is now getting clients in her new business that she's so excited about. She's setting her own boundaries though, now for when she'll work, what she'll do to take care of herself and her health. It's so fun to watch people like that who've become good friends, finally achieve the life they truly desire.

Focusing on your love relationships now will help you get the life YOU truly desire faster. What DO you want out of your life? Where do you want to live? What do you want to be doing for a career, or do you know? Find out! Talk to me or someone who can help you uncover your greatness, your gifts and to find your true passions. These are things to think about and make decisions on so that you can design your ideal lifestyle. You DO have a choice. The grass IS greener if you just open your mind and eyes and see what else is possible for you. You don't have to settle for a job you hate or a person or situation that isn't loving and supportive you know. Don't settle.

You don't even want to tell yourself; "oh it's ok, I'm just waiting 3 years (or more) to be able to retire so I can get my full benefits." That is settling. If you truly are extremely unhappy with what you're doing, you must change quickly. Unhappiness can fester in your body not to mention in your relationships, it can turn to burnout, sickness, negative moods and thoughts, all of it. It's just not healthy.

Let's talk about how you fix it. I'm a fixer. I'm a business coach for entrepreneurs and I'm really good at figuring out where the holes are in someone's business, where they can make a lot more money, where they can get better systems in place to be more efficient and productive and also seeing where the opportunities are, what else is possible for them as far as adding a lot more revenue or streams of income. I'm good at all of that. But when an entrepreneur doesn't tell me that they have a friend, spouse or family member that is causing them harm, distress, stress or worse, then it's hard to fix what I don't know about.

So, let's have you evaluate your relationships, one by one. Let's see if there is something you might be tolerating, or settling around and then see if or how we can fix it. Sit down and really think about every single close relationship you have. What's great about them and then what's not so great, or what's missing?

The love relationship with yourself. Yes, you do need to be "in love" with yourself to be 100% confident in all situations and to be more assertive with what you want and to exude that openness energy that attracts all the right kinds of people. If there are things you may not like that well about yourself such as your body (probably the #1 thing women struggle with), your looks, the lack of boundaries that you may or may not set, the fact that you let people walk all over you perhaps? What are those things that you aren't a fan of? We have to embrace those things, and you might need some professional help in this regard to do this. Know that there are all kinds of people to help you with whatever your struggle is; the best investment you make in your whole life is to get support from any or all of the following depending on what's holding you back.

1. Health coach / Alternative therapist / Hormone specialist / Fitness trainer

2. Emotional eating coach / Nutritionist / Therapist / Image consultant

3. Life coach / Mindset coach / Relationship coach / Transition coach

4. Business coach / Marketing coach / Personal assistant

5. Any number of other professionals... you need to take care of YOU first!

Your relationship with a significant other.

Now, if you don't have one at the moment, you don't want to disregard this section. You want to focus on what you DO want in that next love relationship you'll have. Regardless if you've been divorced, widowed, abandoned, mistreated, or just haven't found the one yet at all, it's ok. There IS someone out there for you and they'll show up when YOU are ready. You may have to work on yourself, however.

When I left my "starter husband" about 16 years ago, it wasn't easy but there hadn't been any intimacy, support or love in our relationship for two years. I won't go into the whole story but we had grown apart and it wasn't going to work. We tried to work it out and it just wasn't going to happen. So, I left, went out on my own, and within a year or so started dating again.

I thought I knew what I wanted in that next love relationship, I had a list of 43 things that described the man I wanted to attract or what our relationship would be like. I thought that I was a great catch and acted as such when I went out on dates. Little did I know that I wasn't ready; I wasn't complete in who I needed to be before attracting that perfect partner for me. It took me five years of painfully dating and being in and out of a couple longer relationships to learn that I had some things I needed to work on! How could that be? I was perfect, it was men who sucked. (ha ha)

Yes, it was true. Some of my female friends recommended I go look up this woman named Allison Armstrong who held these *Understand Men* workshops all over the country. I was fascinated by what I had heard from friends who had been through them. They said they were the best thing since sliced bread. They couldn't rave about them enough.

So, knowing I didn't have much to learn about relationships, I went anyway. The first one blew me away! I learned in fact, that I was totally all screwed up in how I went about my relationships. Yes, the confident, "it's not me, it's you" business coach, was schooled in a big way. I was hooked too. I went to two more workshops of hers before I met the man I'm married to now (my "keeper husband").

The point is that sometimes we don't see what's wrong. Sometimes it's US that needs to change. Sometimes we need to ask for help and support or go take a class, hire someone to help us. We're not born with all the knowledge you will ever need to know in life; we have to learn and continue learning all along our journey.

Here are 8 things I've learned about having a healthy love relationship. I hope this helps you transform your current relationship or find a new and better one.

1. **Talk about money early on**, share your money beliefs, habits, concerns and investment ideas for long-term growth. And do not let someone else fully control the money or have yourself fully control the money. Money is the biggest thing that splits couples apart; make sure you're on the same page when it comes to everything money... especially before you get too deep into the relationship.

2. **Have weekly talks**/meetings about what's going on with everything – jobs, work, kids, money, health, family, needs, goals, etc. Share what your big vision is for your life, and possibly how it's changed since you got together. Share your goals, aspirations and find out theirs. There might be some adjustments you will both need to make in your life to accommodate the other person's new ideas or vision.

3. **Be open to the evolution** of your significant other – they may learn and grow; you either have to learn and grow with them or they may leave you behind.

4. **Set boundaries** around work life and home life and how you raise your kids.

5. **Talk about sex and intimacy**, don't settle. Tell them what you need and want.

6. **Have regular date nights** – don't get out of the habit of doing this. Whether you do these at home or out on the town, you can still make them special – no phones!

7. **Take regular vacations** – whether they are staycations, 3-4-day weekends quarterly to get away or 1-2-week vacations annually, do this. Don't stay stagnant or your relationship will stagnate. It's worth saving for and paying for this stuff, it's critical to long-term happiness and support.

8. **Stay positive when arguing**, don't lash out or use harsh words. Really try to stay calm under pressure, be logical more than emotional. Talk about this when not in an argument too so that you can both be on the same page if something flares up.

Finally, your love relationships with everyone else.

Of course, we love our kids and our parents, but come on, let's face it, sometimes they're challenging. You can use many of the tips above for these types of relationships also but know that most of all, be consistent with them and patient with them. Set boundaries for these relationships also. For kids not to interrupt, do their chores, not bother you if you work from home during certain hours, etc. For parents who might live close by, to still make appointments to come over, not just drop by. Or for those who are needier to talk with them on certain days and times.

Relationships take work, no matter who they are with. Taking the time to nurture each one however will serve you best in the long run.

If you'd like more support around building up your own self-confidence or help get rid of the toxic relationships in your life, go grab my book, *Love Yourself Successful,* online at www.LoveYourselfSuccessful.com today! For more support around starting or growing your business, learn more and access some free business and marketing trainings online at www.JumpstartYourBizNow.com/freetrainings.

About the Author

Katrina Sawa

The JumpStart Your Biz Coach, Katrina Sawa, is the creator of the JumpStart Your Marketing & Sales Systems, and an Int'l Best-Selling author including *Love Yourself Successful* and *Jumpstart Your New Business Now*. She is the CEO of JumpstartYourBizNow.com and JumpstartPublishing.net. Katrina's no-nonsense approach develops consistently profitable businesses implementing proven marketing and business strategies. She's been featured on the Oprah and Friends XMRadioNetwork, ABC, TheCW and dozens of influential podcasts.

Jumpstart Your Money Relationship

5 Steps to a Strong Financial Foundation

By Rev. Andrea Scott Brown

The day I looked up and realized my then-husband and I were $30,000 in debt, my life changed forever. As a teenager and young adult, I was conscious of my money, and I was a "saver". However, I didn't have habits in place to carry me through my marriage. It wasn't until this shock to my system that I became a person on a mission to change my relationship with money.

I wanted to take a stand and change the situation as fast as I could. I went back to work in academia and within a year, we were completely out of debt, except for the house. While my marriage wasn't working, I was recruited by an old boss for a job that would significantly increase my income. It was halfway across the US and I decided to take the job. That precipitated a divorce—fast-tracked in 31 days, and I moved with my kids to our new home on the east coast.

This was a HUGE transition for all of us. What made it a bit easier was the fact that I had changed our financial situation and we were able to land on our feet. I bought a new house in an area with a good school district and close enough to easily commute to work.

I've since stayed out of debt, built wealth, and left corporate again to build my dream of serving others to do the same.

Are you living paycheck to paycheck? Do you let someone else handle the money? Have you had a life event that has made you realize that it is time for you to change your relationship with your money?

When I look back at my journey, I realized I had developed a five-step process that allowed me to change my direction completely and create the life I wanted.

In my coaching business now, I help others change their relationship around money, teaching them what I created. I am all about living your Audacious Path™. And to me, your Audacious Path™ means: Living Your Dream Life. When traveling on your Audacious Path, it is important to take control of your money. When you learn how to use money as a tool and not a stressful burden, your travels are fun, exciting, and fulfilling.

Therefore, the first thing I always do with my clients is to look at your Money Relationship and dig into your financial foundation. We need to figure out what's missing, broken or needing attention.

This is where that 5 Step System to change your relationship with M.O.N.E.Y. comes in. The Steps are:

1. Up-level your Money **Mindset**

2. **Open** the Books

3. Know your **Numbers**

4. **Evaluate** Everything

5. Live on last **Year**'s income

The journey through these five steps can allow you to take control of your money and build a strong financial foundation that you can continue to build and grow. This is just the beginning.

First, to get started on this journey, let's up-level your money mindset. This means looking at your money story. What are your thoughts about money? Do you hear "tapes" or recurring thoughts from your childhood that sound like any of these?

- Money doesn't grow on trees.

- I'm not made of money!

- Rich people don't have hearts.

- Those people are filthy rich.

- Money is dirty.

- A day late and a dollar short.

- You must work HARD for money.

- Money is the root of all evil.

As children, we are all sponges, absorbing all the sights, sounds, experiences, and feelings around us as we grow up. Even if you have heard this before, stop for a moment and think about some of the experiences you had as a child around money. It has shaped how you now relate to money in your everyday life. There are probably many unconscious habits you have developed around how you handle your money, what you purchase, and what you don't.

Now is the time to uncover your "Money Story" and learn what is driving you.

You want to recognize the automatic behaviors and decide if that is how you want to continue. If it isn't, then you have the opportunity to do something different. It's just an experiment. Be curious and see if a new way of spending, tracking, earning, evaluating, or other money behavior would serve you better.

See what happens when you observe your own thoughts and behaviors and get super curious about ways to improve your life. It can be fun!

Next, we get to "Open the Books." This means it's time to find all your money-related information. Go on the hunt for your bank accounts, investments, credit cards, insurance, real estate, retirement, loans, HSAs, and all other assets or liabilities. Gather all the information you can find and keep thinking of others that may have been set aside or forgotten.

This is NOT the time for judgement or criticism about what you may have done in the past or wish you had done. Please remove all judgement and just allow yourself to be the observer. This is the opportunity to move forward from where you are now. Remember, the only constant is change, so the current situation is likely to change very soon. With all this information you are gathering and getting into order, it will likely change for the better.

The third step is to "Know Your Numbers." Now is the time to look at the numbers of the last month, last quarter, last 6 months, and/or last year, and start to understand your spending patterns. When looking at the spending patterns, now you know what types of expenses you've had in the past. You can now set up categories for a spending plan or budget for the future. The plan might be similar to the past or vastly different, you get to decide where to allocate your money. Take control of your money and tell it what you want it to do for you.

I first started with pen and paper to outline my own categories and areas I wanted to track. You can be as detailed or general as you would like to be, just think about what questions you might want to ask when you look back and reflect on your spending. You can always tweak your categories to monitor spending in a new way. For now, just create a draft and know you can change it later. It's better to start with something, anything, so you have something to review.

After pen and paper, I graduated to other tools (go to AudaciousPath.com to find out more) and continued to make changes to my budget and my spending habits to become completely debt-free (except for my house). The key for me was allocating all revenue that came into my life by categories in the budget and then saving to live on last month's income. More on this later.

The fourth step is to "Evaluate Everything." I discovered with my own budget and working with clients' budgets that it takes about three months of actively working with a budget before it becomes somewhat accurate. It takes tweaking and fiddling until it becomes more understandable and relatable to what is *actually* happening each month. Until then, regular meetings with yourself and/or a significant other are required to make changes to the budget after the month begins.

The other part of the evaluation is making decisions about how you want to spend your money including regular reviews of your plan. What subscriptions do you have that are regular/automatic payments that you just pay each time without reviewing the value of the product or service? Look through each one. Do you want to keep it? Do you want to upgrade or downgrade the item? Are you on track for your savings goals, retirement goals, and/or big future purchases? Take time at regular intervals to evaluate where you are now and the progress toward your goals.

Step five is to "Live on Last Year's Income." This may be a far-off goal or not a goal at all. The key is to start living on money already earned, not living paycheck to paycheck. Start by creating a "buffer" that is one paycheck, then two, and move to one full month, so now you are living on last month's income. In this case, you have the money to pay all your bills this month already in the bank ready to pay your bills. As you build this buffer to two months or three months, you have more freedom and flexibility in your financial world. Eventually, you can live on last year's income if that is what you desire. This alone allowed me the freedom to leave my corporate job and build my own business.

Step five is also about creating "Yearly Goals." This helps you review and plan on a larger scale. Now you can see the financial picture on an annual basis and make sure all expenses and goals are covered through the year. Take some time to step back and enjoy the view.

It is easier to work closely with someone who has done this before, however, instead of trying to figure it all out yourself. I would love to be that person for you. I invite you to up-level your money mindset by going to this special page on my website now to get access to a free

Rewrite Your Money Story Guide and an audio training that goes deeper on the M.O.N.E.Y. System as well as the opportunity to have a call with me: www.audaciouspath.com/jumpstart.

With each of these steps, you are closer and closer to taking control of your money, building a strong financial foundation, and changing your relationship with your money.

About the Author

Rev. Andrea Scott Brown

Andrea is an award-winning speaker, author, and coach. She created the Audacious Path™, the M.O.N.E.Y. Course, and the Personal Power Formula™ to help entrepreneurs take control of their money and develop a strong financial foundation. In addition to being a Certified Empowerment Coach, she is also an Infinite Possibilities Certified Trainer and an ordained Metaphysical Minister. When entrepreneurs are on their Audacious Path, they align with their authentic self and true purpose.

Jumpstart Your Radiant Lifestyle

5 Keys to Getting Your Life Back on Track

By Chris Dyer

Have you wondered how some professional women, entrepreneurs and mothers seem to have life in order? They appear organized and make life look neat and easy. Maybe they look like a rock star, hair perfect, moderately fit body, and manage their life schedule like clockwork.

What are some thoughts and triggers that run through your head? Do you get trapped in comparison, envy, and judgement? Do negative emotions of unworthiness or insecurity and lack of courage and confidence occupy your thoughts?

What about those ruminating feelings in your head, heart, and gut that you KNOW you are meant for more? You want more, yet you feel unfulfilled, unsure of your purpose, and seek clarity, focus and direction?

Or your health, lack of energy or motivation has stranded your goals and dreams? You feel stuck, unhappy, unsupported and are riding the roller coaster of emotions.

What is that ONE goal that would change your world? Your family's future? Your career? Imagine the potential of what you will accomplish with a proven strategy of simple habits and consistency... your personal playbook for success.

The life and business of your dreams begin with the decision to change TODAY. A financial adviser would recommend paying yourself or putting aside 10 percent (minimum) of your income consistently for your financial freedom (or both).

Money compounds over time and creates a favorable return for our future. TIME is our most valuable asset (besides ourselves). When we invest 10 percent of our awake hours on our mental, physical, professional, spiritual well-being CONSISTENTLY, we gain control of our future personal and financial health, independence, and resilience. This premise is especially important for caretakers, parents, or nurturing professionals (health care workers, teachers, etc.). The natural tendency is to give all energies to others, without saving for ourselves. Structuring the ten-percent rule into daily habits ensures we fill our cup first, which also helps manage our energy and emotions. To give away

100 percent of your financial abundance would result in being broke.

Do you recognize the parallel of considering time as your best asset? Self-care is the popular buzzword today, which is more than the occasional massage or hours vegetating on social media or a Netflix binge. A radiant lifestyle shift occurs when you effectively manage time to nurture YOUR needs first, which is the basis of getting your life back on **T.R.A.C.K**. (An acronym that I use in my coaching.) The time of day is irrelevant. Your personal success playbook is designed around your life, career and commitments. An exceptional mentor shows you how to minimize excuses, distractions, self-sabotaging behaviors and guides you to set yourself up for personal, professional, and financial WINS!

Now we know that you want more... more confidence, clarity, health, better relationships, money... whatever that is for you. Awareness is always the first step to creating change. Courage to take the next step can be learned and reframed from a fear mindset.

In my Radiant Lifestyle Coaching, I help people get their life back on T.R.A.C.K. which stands for:

- **T**ransforming Thoughts / Mindset / Awareness
- **R**elationships (including self) / Commitment / Invest in Self
- **A**ctions & Habits / Self-Care / Fitness / Nutrition

- **C**areer / Confidence (Image) / Creativity / Passion

- **K**nowing...Trusting that you are on your path to your Radiant Lifestyle!

Transforming old thought patterns, belief systems and expectations handed to you from family and society begins the reprogramming of the new you. I recall early instances when my curiosity allowed me to question 'facts' handed down by family or other respected members of the community. I also remember, as a nine-year-old, when my mother told me that my feelings were not valid and inappropriate. Those two examples clearly represent belief systems (BS) that created YEARS of personal work and reframing so that I could learn to trust and know myself. Clearing out that head trash was essential for me to transcend into a bigger, more impactful version of myself. I am grateful that investing with a coach was the quickest and most effective way through that mire. Are you holding onto old stories that keep you stuck in the quicksand to prevent you from living your radiant life? Your brain is your best friend when you understand how to shape and control your thoughts and dig into your own amazing potential.

The **relationship** you are creating with yourself is the best investment you will ever make. A great mentor will gauge and assess your struggles and desires to design quality questions to help you focus your energy in the best areas for the most effective transformation in the area you are seeking. In the sports world, there are obvious differences in how to train for a marathon vs. how to train for powerlifting. There is an appropriate process for everyone's goal. Weeding out the noise helps define clarity. Are you noticing a trend?

Courage > Clarity > Consistency > Confidence

Three years into my entrepreneur journey as an isolated work-at-home mom of teenagers, I was grateful for the freedom my online business provided around my family schedule and commitments. Additionally, I had successfully created a six-figure income that helped support the household. Always nurturing the needs of the kids' before-and-after-school schedules, plus volunteering left me feeling depleted and my energy and health were dull. I remembered missing how great I felt when participating in aerobics classes ten years earlier.

Acting on my need for more energy and the mental break, I joined a gym and fell in love with a particular dance-style fitness class... it was my gateway into the fitness world. I was HOOKED! I felt alive. My energy returned. My health improved. I lost inches. My mojo came back. And the most important part was I was already FORTY years old... which is important to note that it is NEVER too late to improve your fitness or just get your body moving.

I often would consider myself an introvert and knew that was a trait I wanted to change. During one of the classes I attended, I decided that I wanted to be that instructor on the stage and have that ability to motivate and inspire a room full of energetic ladies through choreography and up-tempo music. That was my next pivotal action step. I jumped in with both feet and completed my first several fitness certifications, including personal training. I created an amazing way to have it all, to work my business around my life, inspire others through a healthy mind and body, and still honor those important parts of my habits today.

My goal is to inspire YOU to act! Through years of gradual transformation and doing the work, I have formulated simple concepts into tangible and teachable habits and bite-sized chunks. There are options for everyone I work with or inspire throughout my coaching, even when working with the senior groups in some of my fitness classes. Our habits TODAY influence and shape our future selves. To LOVE yourself today, even if you are not yet sure what that looks like is making the best decision towards loving your future and independence and what you imagine that to be. I invite you to close your eyes for 30 seconds and imagine yourself at 75 or 80 years old.

Where are you? Who are you with? What are you doing? It is never too late to change your trajectory (remember, I started the *consistent* healthy journey at 40) to start today and begin living the radiant life you can imagine...with zest and confidence.

Throughout the past 30+ years, my peers and tribe have curiously inquired and observed how I manage(d) life, career, education, working four part-time jobs in my past just to make the mortgage payment. How do I have the energy to show up, roll up my sleeves and dig into the various roles I enjoy? I have mastered how to manage and focus my desires and create my own renewable sources of energy, **confidence** (by acting), embracing my inherent **creativity** along my career paths.

The bold words throughout this chapter are my gifts to inspire you to decide what is next for you and ask yourself the tough questions. I am always open to challenging myself (and you) to think and act more boldly. What can I or should I be doing that will move me in the direction of my goals and dreams?

When you **know** what you want and are ready and willing to put in the work, you will begin to trust yourself. You become the CEO of your life and your own soul mate or best friend. You begin to love yourself and live your life within YOUR values, alignment, and integrity. Everything you aspire to becomes more within your reach. Your relationships flourish. Your career, creativity, and passion blossoms. And there is nothing that replaces **knowing** yourself, your worth, and your contribution to the people you love and the lives you touch.

You already possess the power to control your next best decision. If you have been inspired by anything shared in these few pages, my door is open. **I invite you to go to my website at**
www.JumpstartYourRadiantLifestyle.com
and get access to a free one-on-one call with me plus my video training on the 5 Steps to Getting Your Life Back on T.R.A.C.K.!

It's time to Jumpstart Your Radiant Life!

About the Author

Chris Dyer

Chris Dyer is a Courage and Confidence Coach with over 30+ years of combined education and experience. She is the founder and CEO of two marketing and branding start-ups and attributes success to staying on T.R.A.C.K. to build the life of her dreams. She enthusiastically continues to serve her community through health & fitness lifestyle and volunteers for many civic groups and local and international networking organizations.

By Chris Dyer

Jumpstart
Your Business
Chapters

Jumpstart Your Brand

How to Build an Irresistible Brand that Turns Heads Everywhere

By Rhonda Swan

The internet is a packed, noisy place. From startups to behemoth eCommerce brands, from mom-and-pop shops to Fortune 500 companies, from bloggers to affiliate marketers; everyone is jostling for attention. Only through smart personal branding can you stand out from the competition and get noticed.

Thanks to the internet and supersonic technological advancements anyone anywhere can make money online.

Yes, you too.

Not only can you supplement your regular income through a lucrative side hustle but you can also make six figures or more from the comfort of your home.

Armed only with a laptop, an internet connection, a solid idea, and plenty of gumption, you can build a global personal brand.

By the end of 2020, global eCommerce sales reached a mouth-watering $4.2 billion.

With online shopping becoming more popular as shoppers get more comfortable shopping on mobile devices, online commerce sales will balloon to $6.54 billion by 2023.

That's a tremendous opportunity for solo entrepreneurs and online fortune hunters.

I'm sure you also want some.

But with everyone jostling for a piece of the cake, the competition is fierce. Gaining attention online has become tougher than ever.

That's where personal branding comes in to save the day. This in-depth guide will teach you everything you need to know about personal branding so you position your company favorably, get noticed, and win business despite the stiff competition.

What is Personal Branding?

Personal branding is the deliberate effort to create, shape, and manage public perception of a person and what they stand for. It's an ongoing process that seeks to position the individual as an industry authority, boost their credibility, and differentiate them from the competition.

Ultimately, smart personal branding gives you a competitive edge, increases your influence and earnings on the market because of the positive impression people have about you.

5 Crucial Brand Identity Basics

1. **Logo:** A logo is a symbol or mark that identifies a unique business entity. A superb logo grabs attention and helps people to understand what a business does or represents fast.

   There are four main types of logos:

   - **Wordmark or Logotype** - this is a text-only logo, a good fit if your company has a short name. Google has this type of logo.

   - **Monogram** - this is a 1 to 3 letter logo, where a company uses its initials as the logo.

   - **Brandmark logo** - this is an icon or picture logo, this is risky if you aren't yet known. Apple

Computers uses a Brandmark logo with their "apple".

- **Combination logo** - as the name implies, this type of logo merges wordmark, monogram and brandmark into one logo. Doritos uses a combination logo.

When you are starting, you may be tempted to spend a lot of time and financial resources crafting the perfect logo. Don't get hung up on your logo. Just come up with something simple and affordable in the beginning. You can always change it later when your brand identity has crystallized.

2. **Tagline:** A tagline is a punchy catchphrase or slogan that conveys the value you provide. Your tagline supports your logo in describing the essence of your brand. It also acts as a differentiation factor by capturing your unique value. For inspiration on how to craft a sticky tagline, consider these case studies:

- M&M's "Melts in your mouth, not in your hands."
- KFC "It's finger-licking good."
- Apple "Think different."
- There are 3 elements of an unforgettable slogan: Simple, Unique and Aligned

3. **Color Schemes:** Colors are powerful. They make a deep psychological impact on us. Color influences

our behavior more than we realize or care to admit. For instance, did you know that up to 93% of consumers consider mostly visual factors when making purchase decisions? Color also increases brand recognition by 80%. Limit your colors to one or two for clarity. Having too many brand colors confuses your audience.

To get you thinking about your brand colors, here are 7 colors and their meaning.

- Red: boldness, youthfulness, excitement.
- Black: luxury, classy, sophistication.
- Purple: royalty, extravagance, creativity.
- White: purity, goodness, safety.
- Green: nature, health, growth.
- Blue: intelligence, dependability, security.
- Orange: happiness, friendliness, courage.

4. **Mission Statement:** A mission statement is a succinct description that sums up the purpose, values, and goals of your brand. Like the tagline, your mission statement helps distinguish your brand from the countless companies out there.

Here are some quick tips on coming with a brilliant mission statement:

- Keep it straightforward for painless comprehension.

- Avoid gobbledygook and buzzwords that sound fancy but communicate nothing, e.g. core-competency, buy-in, cutting-edge, market-leader, etc.

- Focus on how your business benefits your audience in the long run.

- Zero in on what makes you different from your competitors.

- Tell a brief, inspiring story that outlines what you do fascinatingly.

- Brevity is key because you are not writing an essay.

To prime your creativity pump as you craft your mission statement, here are three examples of inspirational vision statements.

First up is Ann Handley.
"Empowering ridiculously good marketing."
It's simple and delicious.

Next is billionaire Oprah Winfrey.
"To be a teacher. And to be known for inspiring my students to be more than they thought they could be."

Lastly, let's look at JetBlue's mission statement.
"To inspire humanity–both in the air and on the ground. We are committed to giving back in meaningful ways in the communities we serve and to inspire others to do the same."

Yes, JetBlue isn't a personal brand, but its vision statement is exceptional. It's a perfect example of an audience-centered mission statement laden with benefits while still communicating company values in one stroke. Your mission statement announces to the world why your company exists, your voice and style are how you say it.

5. **Voice and Style:** Brand voice and style is how you come across when you communicate.

   Your values and mission are the substance of your brand—your brand voice and style are the sizzle. Your logo, tagline, goals, and mission make up the base of your brand pizza, voice and style are the scrumptious toppings.

   No matter how marvelous your mission and products are, without an appealing voice, you will struggle to attract customers. Look at the chart below that shows four brand voices your brand can adopt: passionate, quirky, irreverent, and authentic.

For your brand voice to stick, it must permeate everything you do. Who you are and whom you serve determines your voice. Be comfortable in your skin. Use an authentic voice that makes sense to you and your target audience in a business context.

It's time to raise your voice. Your tribe or best potential clients are eagerly waiting to hear it and come running.

Let me remind you of a popular business mantra: People do business with people they know, love, and trust.

That's exactly why a personal brand is powerful. Because people do business with people, not faceless corporations. Even in vast organizations, there are faces of the brand who are instantly recognizable. Their audience connects with the brand through them.

Here are four benefits of a personal brand.

1. **Boosts Your Company's Credibility:** Personal brands exude warmth, intimacy, and authenticity. Unlike massive operations that seem fake, personal brands appear more authentic. Whether it's because of being familiar with one person they deal with often or getting personal attention, people love the credibility of personal brands.

2. **Increases Brand Visibility:** A well-optimized online personal brand boosts your business's visibility. When people Google services or products related to what you do, your brand turns up. Since most product searches start with a Google search, your customers can only increase. But it's a double-edged sword. This is because you are the brand, any slip-ups morally or otherwise will mar your brand's reputation.

3. **Helps You Stand Out from Competitors:** Humans are distinct. Of the 7,874,965,825 people alive on the globe today, nobody looks like you or has your exact personality. So, if you package your brand correctly around your identity, you will be a unique brand; Special, Ravishing, Unrivaled. As long as you stay true to your identity, your brand will have an aura of va-va-voom nobody can challenge.

4. **Attract Your Ideal Customers:** No appeals to everyone. Too many entrepreneurs use a one-size-fits-all marketing approach. They try to make everyone their customer. If you aim to persuade everyone to become your customer, you won't reach anyone. Your message will be too generic, lifeless, and powerless. On the flip side, if you go after a particular slice of the market with people who share the same values as you, your message will resonate. They will buy from you and follow you everywhere.

In addition, a story coming from a respectable 3rd party source will establish your company's authority and positioning in your industry and spread the good word about what you're doing.

Having quality PR and media is critical for a company's growth, development and brand positioning. At my company, the Unstoppable Branding Agency, we focus on turning "best-kept secrets" into "worlds known experts."

Helping our clients create media connections that build trust with their audience and increase credibility and revenue is what we do.

After spending nearly a decade working in PR and marketing for fortune 100 companies and multi-million-dollar brands and startups, I know what truly drives conversions, sold-out launches and how to get my clients featured in Top Tier Publications.

If you would like to talk with me about how we can possibly Jumpstart Your Brand and your business in the process, please go to my website at www.UnstoppableBrandingAgency.com today and submit a request. Or you can follow us on Facebook or Instagram.

Now, go transform your brand into one people remember. You are unstoppable!

About the Author

Rhonda Swan

Rhonda is the CEO of the Unstoppable Branding Agency, the top global PR & branding firm for entrepreneurs rated by Forbes Magazine. She is also the founder of the Women Gone Wild, the world's largest women empowerment movement and Book Series. She has been featured in Forbes, Entrepreneur, and INC Magazines and was named the Top Women to Watch in 2021 by Fast Company. After spending nearly a decade working in PR and marketing for fortune 100 companies and multimillion-dollar brands and startups, Rhonda knows what truly drives brand positioning, sales conversions, sold-out launches, and how to get her clients featured in Top Tier Publications.

Jumpstart Your Business

3 Critical Keys to Becoming Profitable

By Katrina Sawa

As a business and marketing coach, I see thousands of small business owners struggling every year and that breaks my heart.

They struggle to generate consistent cash flow. They struggle to find a balance between work and family or personal time. They struggle often with decisions relating to their business, marketing, growth and more.

Let's face it; it's not easy being a small business owner. It hasn't been easy for me; that's for sure. We don't know what we don't know, right?

I'm constantly learning, listening, testing and putting myself out there.

When I first decided to start my business back in 2002, I was working as a Marketing Director at an Assisted Living Facility. I had only been there for 6 months and I knew this wasn't the right industry for me. Moreover, my boss was not someone I could trust or count on either which didn't help.

Before that job, I had sold advertising for the local newspaper, a job I really grew to love. I loved meeting and interacting with the small businesses I came in contact with each month. They had real passion, drive and perseverance. The problem was that they didn't have a lot of marketing and sales training!

I saw businesses going out of business often, too often. It was so sad. I realized back then that I knew a LOT about marketing and selling and I could help them with more than just selling them ad space.

When I told my "starter husband" that I wanted to start my own business doing marketing consulting, he "said" he was supportive but as it turns out, he wasn't really.

As it turns out he had more of a scarcity mentality and I didn't know it. I was more of a risk-taker looking back, a true entrepreneur; he was not. I refer to this as Entrepreneur vs. Employee Mindsets - they are very different. Typically, you find these two types married too, which without the proper communication, can really harm a relationship.

Well, you guessed it, we ended up getting a divorce. I wasn't willing to go back and get a job after I got the taste of being my own boss and he wasn't willing to learn more about my true purpose, passions and goals. Ultimately, it was a really great decision to break up because having someone who really doesn't believe in you or isn't 100% supportive of you can really harm your entrepreneurial spirit and we need that positive spirit with us constantly because it takes a lot to maintain our confidence and motivation.

After the divorce, I was free of negativity, but I still had a big road ahead of me to really get where I am today and where I still want to be.

I had a bout with my own ego in the early days too. I thought I knew what to do and didn't always heed the advice of those ahead of me or even some of the mentors that I paid!

Then of course, it's the constant doubt that creeps in and tells you things like: "who are you to charge that or do that?", "you're not good enough" and "insert YOUR head trash in here".

So how do we combat these thoughts, feelings and emotions that can daily sabotage our productivity, motivation, and success?

Well, I've learned a few things in the past few years that helped me and maybe they'll help you too.

Are you ready to scale your business or take it to the next level and fast?

Whether you're newer in business or you've been in business a while now... we all have a "next level" we strive to achieve.

I want to share with you the 3 Critical Keys to becoming more consistently profitable that I've found have been instrumental with my own life and motivation.

I came up with these one day listening to another speaker share a story in his talk. He was talking about how we, as speakers, choose what we speak about, what our signature talk and/or stories will be.

He said something that felt like a challenge to me that day. He said: "you're on a plane, it's going down, you're not going to make it but the person next to you is. What is it that you tell the person sitting next to you about what you do, what are the most critical things, they need to know?"

That made me really sit up and think, "Wow, what are those critical aspects of being an entrepreneur that someone really needs to know?" As I reflected on that, and really thought about summing them up into 3 things or less, this is what I came up with. It's a different way of looking at business perhaps but hear me out.

1. **Be Love**

2. **Be Organized**

3. **Always Be Marketing**

Be Love

First, you really need to learn how to BE. How to just be open to what's possible, be open to who needs what you've got, be open to who you are and how you can best serve. Be open and listen to your intuition, your gut, as to what to charge, offer and decide to take on in your business.

The love part comes in because you will need to give yourself grace at times, give yourself permission, love, and courage. BEing love means to go with the flow and stop pushing and just start receiving.

I will admit that this was really hard for me to do back in 2008 when I was first introduced to this idea of BEing, being love. I was in a high-end mastermind with a mentor I had at the time and about 14 of my peers and friends. I would attend the mastermind retreats where we were supposed to all get a "hot seat" session focused on our businesses and everyone would give us feedback on what they thought we could do or improve upon. Well, I went to those meetings ready to rock and roll, asking for what I could do to grow my revenues, build the business, that sort of thing. Yet all my peers and my mentor would offer me was to "just BE Katrina, BE love".

I was completely frustrated, to say the least, after all, I was all about the doing. I was good at completing tasks, getting shit done. I was not good at stagnation, and that's what I felt like they were saying to me at the time. "Just sit around and do nothing, Katrina" is what I felt like they were saying.

But I wanted to get to that $100,000 mark in my business that year!! How the heck was I supposed to do that just "being"?

Well, it's funny really, because it worked. I DID hit $100,000 that year in revenues and I didn't DO anything additional or different. I would just BE, when I went to events and conferences. I would wait to see who was drawn to me, and I would give them all the advice I could openly and freely. People wanted more. They appreciated the fact that I was so open to giving and pouring into them, that they wanted more.

Although I cried all year long thinking this advice of BEing wasn't doing anything for me, it did work. And today, 11 years later, I'm still reminding myself to BE rather than always DO. You can do this too... try it!

Be Organized

Being organized seems really straight forward, but I assure you, there is a LOT to it when you think about all aspects of business life. You need to learn how to be strategically organized in ALL of the following to be super successful in my mind:

- Your big picture business and marketing planning, including what to do with your random awesome ideas that come up!

- Your physical space: office, desk, files, paper, etc. If you do not have a dedicated space for you to work freely without distractions, this will be a challenge for you. Give yourself the gift of a dedicated workspace please.

- Your electronic space: computer and laptop files, folders, client documents, marketing materials, photos, etc. plus in your phone, email database, shopping cart, payment gateway, website pages, backend functionality, other techy tools you use and a whole lot more. If you are not a techy person, this will be your biggest challenge!

- Your marketing: what you'll post, share, send, speak weekly, daily, monthly. Will you have themes? How to stay consistently in front of your ideal prospects and clients.

- Your launches and offerings, what you'll sell when.

- Your daily tasks and to-dos.

- What you delegate to your team and when.

- Your finances, where you put the money you make, how you manage and track it, spend it, etc.

- Your schedule, calendar and how you manage your time. We only have so much time in the day, if you're not highly productive, you will work way too hard and long. (See the chapter on Jumpstarting Your Productivity in this book for more tips.)

Do you have challenges staying organized? If so, you need to hire help for this as soon as possible! If you drown in disorganization, it will hold you back tremendously. I call it, Manual Labor Chaos; it's when you're in the weeds or overwhelmed with too much to do. It's usually because you haven't gotten organized enough or you haven't delegated properly or enough to a team yet.

The good news is that getting more organized can be learned or hired out. I often look into my clients' laptops or computers and show them how to name files or organize their folders so they can find things easier. I even had a professional organizer client who is amazing with physical spaces but not too techy, who didn't realize she could organize her electronic files into folders on her computer! Now, you might think that's a simple task, but the point is that you just don't know what you don't know. And when someone like me can point out those "holes" in your business, and we show you how to tweak them, it can make the world of difference in your efficiency but also your bottom line.

Always Be Marketing

This seems simple too to some. Post on social media, right?

No, that is NOT all you have to do these days. In fact, I have a new theory that I teach at my events and to clients and it's about "picking a lane".

You see, there are two types of people, right? Introverts and Extroverts. Generally speaking, Introverts prefer staying behind their computers doing their marketing online while Extroverts like to get in front of groups of people through speaking, networking, events and talking more individually one-on-one.

Now, I know that's a generalization and Introverts also speak and network, just like us Extroverts do online marketing. However, these days with a dozen or so well-known, online social media platforms and hundreds of others less known or that are run more privately, you simply can't be everywhere and do a good job at being seen in all those places. You should really pick a couple of platforms that you'll focus on if you choose this lane. But for online marketing like social media, you have to literally create, feed and engage in your groups/communities daily, multiple times a day! It's exhausting for me actually to spend my time that way, I much prefer to attend and speak at events, in person or on Zoom. However, many entrepreneurs love that type of business model and marketing.

Which do you prefer?

If you choose the speaking, networking lane, then you need to do THAT weekly if not daily to grow and build your business. It is pretty impossible to do both really well, so I say "pick a lane" and excel there. Ingrain yourself in that lane... be known like crazy in the lane you choose. Then do the minimum in the other lane to stay visible.

Each lane requires an action plan, strategies and tactics that you'll implement each week. What you don't want to do is "wing it", trying things out randomly but not consistently. That won't work and you'll waste a lot of precious time and money without results.

Give yourself permission NOT to do it all when it comes to your marketing, you can thank me later.

Regarding the "always" in Always Be Marketing... what do I mean by that?

That means always being observant for any opportunity to talk about or showcase your business or expertise. Many entrepreneurs don't think like a "marketer" and you need to. Doing so doesn't make you annoying, pushy or salesy, but it does give you an advantage because you'll recognize more opportunities that many miss or are too busy to take advantage of.

Always Be Marketing means when you're out and about on the weekend, have your business cards on hand in case you spark up a conversation with someone who could use your products and services.

It means having your books if you have books, with you when you travel on a plane, possibly sticking some in the backs of the plane seats or in bookstores for "Reverse Shoplifting".

It means when you see someone looking for guests for a podcast or articles for a magazine or blog that you STOP what you're doing, and apply or send something in to be considered. You put yourself out there in any opportunity that comes along if it's something that will elevate you as an expert and/or reach your ideal prospects.

If things have become stagnant in your business then it could be time to see if any of these three crucial areas in your business could use some attention. Many people come to me who've been in business for several years and they've made a certain amount of money, but then they are **STUCK**! They don't know what to change; is it their business model, marketing or structure? They don't know what they don't know. They want more but aren't sure how to get there. They can't see what to implement, add or delete to their marketing and strategy to take their business to the next level.

If you'd like to have a conversation to review your Big Vision, Marketing or Business Strategy, Organization, and more, to see what I can suggest for you to **take YOUR business to the next level and fast**, then go sign up for a complimentary business planning session with me. This session is totally free for those of you reading this chapter but please don't wait, life is way too short to WAIT for more success and happiness. **Sign up now at www.JumpstartYourBizNow.com/FreeCallWithKat.**

Keep in mind that if your goal is making $100,000 or less, it doesn't end up being enough when you get there, at least that's what I learned. Even at $200,000 per year in revenues, I wanted more, you will too. Once you see what's possible and once you build a team to support you, your big vision gets bigger! You'll want more too. You'll want more for yourself, your family, your clients and the world. Dream bigger, play bigger and you can make a really big impact!

About the Author

Katrina Sawa

The JumpStart Your Biz Coach, Katrina Sawa, is the creator of the JumpStart Your Marketing & Sales Systems, and an Int'l Best-Selling author including *Love Yourself Successful* and *Jumpstart Your New Business Now*. She is the CEO of JumpstartYourBizNow.com and JumpstartPublishing.net. Katrina's no-nonsense approach develops consistently profitable businesses implementing proven marketing and business strategies. She's been featured on the Oprah and Friends XMRadioNetwork, ABC, TheCW and dozens of influential podcasts.

Jumpstart your Community

How to Cultivate an Engaged Business Community

By Colleen Biggs

Have you ever felt you were meant for something more? That your intuition was telling you to pioneer your own path? Yeah, me too! And it all started here...

My years in Corporate America seemed to be the right fit as I climbed the ladder to Executive leadership. Coaching CEOs through the launch of their businesses and beyond fueled my drive for excellence. I mastered Servant Leadership and shared my knowledge with everyone I came in contact with. I took on anything and everything within work and my personal life that involved giving back through service. My heart was full of gratitude for this opportunity to fulfill my leadership opportunities. I even achieved a 1st degree in the practice of Taekwondo. Yet, there was still something missing. Que self-discovery 2.0!

I traveled 80% of the month during my last 24 months with my corporate position. Spending several hours at a time in a car or plane was not uncommon, so I took to listening and learning the audible way! **Let me repeat... have you ever felt you were meant for something more? That your intuition was telling you to pioneer your own path?** These were the continuous thoughts as I navigated my way through 48 states. Each visit with clients, every discussion had, brought me closer to my destiny; People, Stories, Listening, Showing Up, Validation, Confidence, and Bingo! This is why I'm here! My mind volcano erupted with visions, thoughts, ideas, and plans that were so vivid. Even today, I'm overwhelmed by the thought of the clarity I was offered at that moment. My path was to create a community that provided women the exposure to share all of this!!! The Lead Up for Women seeds were planted.

When women are together in a community they succumb to hierarchy and simply support and connect. Change begins.

Fast forward to 6 months before the ah-ha moment! I was attending a retreat where women come together in the commercial construction industry for business development. I had attended this once in the past but this time, it was different. I was able to clearly see as if the optometrist had handed me glasses for the first time, how each woman possessed her own unique power in her approach to her position. I could feel the power in the room; the sense of support for her fellow sisters and the thread of connection for the understanding of how difficult it can be for women in this industry. Was it really only for women in the Construction industry? Heck no! It was for all women! Women in IT, healthcare, finance, and every other industry of business.

I'm going to change the world was what I said to myself when the roundtable session ended. And the journey to empower women to show up and lean into their purpose began! You see, that day, in that room, every woman showed up! They felt safe in the community, let down their guard for a moment and became vulnerable with the others.

"Never doubt that a small group of thoughtful, committed citizens can change the world; indeed, it's the only thing that ever has." - Margaret Mead

The business plan building began the week after the event in August of 2018. Just a short 4 months later, Lead Up for Women was launched. During those 4 months, I walked purposefully through the branding process to create a vision, mission and core values. This is essential when launching a business as you need to ensure you have the correct messaging and are presenting a solution to a problem that exists in the world today. Women not showing up as themselves and unleashing their power is a problem and the platforms that Lead Up for Women offer is the solution.

Here are 6 key initial steps to take when launching a community:

1. **The boring business stuff:** Involve an attorney if you are starting a business and ensure you are filing the correct entity for the community you want to create. Open a business bank account if you intend to collect money for memberships to be part of this community.

2. **Ensure the community is needed and solves a problem that exists in society today.** People are more willing to join when they know *what's in it for me*! I live by this. W.I.I.F.M.

3. **Market!** Reach out to everyone and anyone you have connected with in the past to involve them in your mission. Tell everyone about what you are doing. Share your passion and enroll them! Did I mention calling everyone? Yes, everyone!

4. **Start a podcast or an online live show weekly!** Get the word out quickly that you are building this community and many more will join as you share your passion for *WHY* you created the community in the first place.

5. **Have a MISSION!!!** Set a goal for how many members you wish to have and why.

6. **Nurture your contacts!** This means care about them, ask them what they want and deliver!

Put in the work: Research, research, research! *We have over 3.4 million listeners and the majority of them are* *women,* they said. *"Where do I sign,"* I stated. The next chapter, Lead Up for Women hits the radio waves. I'll be honest, being a radio show host was never on my mind and was not a vision I had for Lead Up.

At the time we were offered the show, I was still working at corporate, traveling for business, launching our first edition of Lead Up for Women magazine, launching our luncheon series across the nation and I was teaching fitness classes weekly in my local community. However, I couldn't resist the temptation when VoiceAmerica® asked us to lead their Women Series they were launching on the Empowerment channel.

So, I stayed up night after night listening to podcasts, researching how to interview, what to ask, what not to say, who to invite on your show, how to market, and everything else you can imagine it takes to be a successful radio show host! This went on for about a month until I felt prepared enough to step into the studio. This platform we have today allows us to share women's stories. These stories inspire and motivate our global listeners. It gives them the permission they seek and need to tap into their superpower and lean into their purpose, write their stories and fulfill their dreams. How grateful I am to all of the amazing women I have had the pleasure of interviewing and will interview in the future.

What's your superpower?

Having the energy to endure many projects at once and to show up like me, every time, and in every situation is my superpower. I see others for exactly who they are, without judgement, good and bad. You'll remember from earlier in the chapter that I didn't always know that was mine, but just as a pearl is born from a grain of sand, I too was *born* from the grit that entered my world. Showing up for women and having the events platform is certainly one of my favorite legs of Lead Up! Dig deep and learn what lights you up, then activate it!!! Build your community around that Superpower!

Over the past 20 years or so, I have nurtured and grown my contact lists. Doing this for so many years proved to be the catalyst and foundation for a successful launch. I regularly reach out to individuals and personally invite my contacts to the events through phone calls, LinkedIn invites, personal emails, and text messages. **If you don't have a strong contact list, I would recommend creating one!** I talk to everyone I meet for two reasons; to learn their story and gather their contact information to see how I can assist them in connecting with the thousands of contacts I know.

When your mission is to change the world, one person at a time, you look for every opportunity to do so, even on a plane!

The journey with the Lead Up for Women Community has been more gratifying than I ever imagined. Women all over the world connect with us through our online media and radio. They receive our newsletters, comment on our website, submit and read articles for the bi-monthly magazine and have become part of a community of women that lift, support, accept, contribute, endorse, and love one another. There are a plethora of reasons to support why it's impossible to create change in this world, especially from a child that believed she was not worth $100 per month.

If you're interested in learning about the Lead Up for Women community, and how you too can create a community to support your mission, **head over to www.ColleenBiggs.net/jumpstart to get a whole host of free gifts I would love for you to have.** These free resources will empower you to expand your influence and build a community:

- 6 key initial steps to take when launching a community
- Free Invite to the next Lead Up for Women Lunch-N-Learn
- Free 30-min Build your Community Strategy Call with me
- Free Digital Lead Up for Women Magazine

Finally, believe in you and believe it's possible, and you too can pick up the pen and write your story and create a community strong enough to create everlasting change. Your future is waiting. Start the community you have always dreamed of now!

About the Author
Colleen Biggs

Colleen Biggs is an Award-Winning Peak Performance Consultant, has over 20 years of experience, launched over 340 businesses, an International Speaker, Author, CEO of three businesses, including Lead Up for Women, a community that boasts tens of thousands of female entrepreneurs driven by their passions, support and promote others with a purpose to fuel female voices with power that are leading the way for all female Entrepreneurs Worldwide.

Jumpstart Your Productivity

Using Systems and Technology for More Sales and Freedom

By Katrina Sawa

People always ask me, "How do you do so much and make it all look so easy?"

What I've discovered in my 19+ years of being an entrepreneur is that the productivity practices I've adopted or developed are some of the most important systems that have helped me get to where I am in my business today.

Using systems and consistent ways to market and follow up is entirely how I built my multiple six-figure business. It wasn't always that easy, however; I had to learn the hard way.

I am a recovering control freak myself and tried to do it all myself for the first few years but I got burned out and even got divorced along the way. I felt like I knew enough to figure out this entrepreneur thing; I had a business degree with a marketing concentration but I was sorely mistaken. My ego got in the way for about four or five years in fact, until I finally took my mentors' advice.

About nine months into my business, I had to ask my mom to come in and help me update my QuickBooks because I was super unorganized with my receipts and books and she was experienced in this area. She fixed it all then said: "Now you need to hire a bookkeeper because I'm not coming back."

The first time I tried to hire an assistant, I hired a young intern that worked in my home office with me and I would stand over him peering onto his laptop, critiquing his work as he went along. That is NOT a productive way to hire and manage your people!

These days, I find it much less stressful and enjoyable to delegate, have systems in place, great functionality on my website so I can attract, talk to and help thousands of more entrepreneurs than I ever could before with my old business model and practices.

I use templates for just about everything and I clone previous work to complete new work such as emails, webpages and articles.

For my marketing tasks, like email marketing, follow up, direct mail, social media connecting and more; I use systematized lead generation strategies and my team to get more visible and reach a lot more people. If I did manually what my team and our automation do for me every week, I'd never sleep. You have to embrace technology, team and systems to get farther faster in your business.

The 5 areas to focus on to get more productive are:

1. Templates
2. Systems
3. Outsourcing
4. Technology
5. Scheduling

There is so much you can do online to market and promote your business but no ONE entrepreneur can ever do it all, at least not effectively of course.

Therefore, you must learn how to automate as much of your business and marketing tasks as humanly possible. You need to do this though without compromising your relationships or much-needed personal touch, however.

Most entrepreneurs barely reach 5-10% of the potential number of prospects they could with what they attempt to accomplish in their marketing efforts. You can be in many more places and be much more well known if you learn some simple techniques for automating, delegating and systematizing much of what you do.

Here are just a few ideas you can look at in your business to see if or how you can automate:

1. Your online business set up

   a. You need a **professionally designed website** for credibility. Please don't build your website yourself unless you're a trained website developer with a lot of sales and marketing experience.

   b. You want to **offer a freebie** (or two or three) that your visitors can sign up to receive. On every page of your website, you'll put an opt-in box that stands out like a sore thumb (Getting people on your email list is the #1 goal of your website!).

   c. Most business owners should have **shopping carts** hooked up to their website so people can click and buy but also to house your database and to send your database email newsletters, promotions and more. There is an exhausting number of platforms you can use frankly, please ask for advice on this from more than one person and evaluate each based on what YOU need for YOUR type of business. Most entrepreneurs I see are paying for too many online software platforms and services when they could simplify with one or two that would be sufficient to run their entire business, but you don't know what you don't know.

d. You may want **online forms, FAQ pages, video tutorials** or online quizzes or assessments to get people interacting on your site. If you don't get them interacting pretty quickly, they'll leave. This is a must!

e. Learn how to write really effective **website copy** and content, this will make or break your results. Most entrepreneurs should take classes on this as it doesn't come naturally. You have to take your online visitors through a process of discovering more about you and your services while giving them solutions for what they're searching for.

2. Your marketing and follow up

a. Develop a **pre-consultation questionnaire or intake form** online to help qualify prospects and have them take the initiative. Put this on your website though, everything should go in and through your website.

b. Create **printed order forms** to take to in-person networking events and conferences – get prospects while they're hot! Enter their information later. Sometimes using technology on the spot works, but oftentimes, it creates more manual labor in the back end.

c. **Pre-write emails** and mailings for follow-up after networking events so you aren't recreating the wheel. This is definitely something you can delegate!

d. **Check your voice mail** to make sure it's professional

and effective – tell callers what to do, go online, get freebies, email you, etc.

e. Put a full email signature together with a link to your freebies in the P.S. everywhere you can, on email replies, social media direct messages and more.

3. Your life

    a. Hire a housekeeper, nanny, landscaper or errand service.

    b. Shop online and pay bills online.

Those are just a few things to get you started but if you understand that you can increase your business with more automating, delegating and systematizing, then I highly recommend you ask for help to get more focused and organized in your business.

We can be overwhelmed with our business, our to-do lists, our email, social media, our prospecting and follow up - so much that none of it gets done right? Have you ever been so stuck on what to do that you can't do anything productive at all?

Well, when (or if) that happens to you, I hope you stop to think first:

"What's the big goal that I'm trying to achieve? What are the most productive things I can do to get me there?"

This could be a personal or business goal; either way, there is an order in which you want to do things to ensure you get to the result you want. You want to prioritize those things and hold yourself accountable (or get someone else to hold you accountable) and get to work.

It's especially tough to prioritize and get stuff done if life throws you a curveball, such as; issues in your relationship, a death or sickness in the family, a child moving out to college or some other life-changing or tragic occurrence.

How are you supposed to focus or get things done then?

Having systems and at least a small team will help maintain normal business, marketing and sales tasks while you take whatever necessary time off. Without proper effective systems or team members, your revenue could take a nosedive for sure... and for how long?

In your business, you will have ups and downs. You will have successes and failures. You will have big boosts of revenue and big valleys of nothing at some point.

What I've found is that most entrepreneurs are not taking the time to work "on" their businesses, they only struggle and stress out "in" it.

These same entrepreneurs are not open to learning new techniques about marketing, learning new industry standards, keeping their website and marketing materials current or even getting out and meeting new people to build relationships with to further their business. Or it may be that they're open to it but they don't see it as a necessary enough thing to fit into their schedule.

Hopefully, this doesn't sound familiar to you. But if it does....

Here are 10 ways to get more productive immediately:

1. **Schedule 1 day each month as "Creative" Day** - a day you will do nothing but sit and write down all the ideas that come to mind about how you can update or increase your business, who you know that you can work with on joint ventures, etc.

2. **Schedule another day each month as "Implement" Day** - a day you will do nothing but put those ideas into action - updating the text on your websites, writing and sending out a press release, planning your next workshop with flyer development, etc.

3. **Plot in your calendar every month the things that move the needle** such as networking events, marketing conferences, calls with referral sources, lead-generating tasks such as webinars, interviews, videos live on social media and more. Don't let other things get in the way of these necessary business-building strategies.

4. **Work off a good calendar system** that can help you track your time. Plot blocks of time out for different activities and one that you can use anywhere you are to save time (i.e.; Google Calendar).

5. **Track your time for one week solid** on everything you do, personally and professionally, and see where you're wasting time, could get rid of things you're doing, delegate or automate some things you're doing, etc.

6. **Set goals for yourself each day**, week and month on what you plan to accomplish making sure that you don't take on too huge of a goal, such as "write my book". Instead, take a chunk of that larger project and do part of it so it's easier to accomplish.

7. **Find an accountability buddy** (or coach) or someone who supports what you're doing in your business fully to stay in touch with however often you need them too – daily, weekly or monthly perhaps but that may be too long.

8. **Unsubscribe from emails and lists** that are slowing you down and not contributing to either your enhanced learning, implementing, taking action or accountability. Or have them redirect into a folder you won't see every day and you can look at when you have time. But don't let daily emails distract you from the tasks at hand.

9. **Have a marketing and business plan** that you're working from so you know WHERE and HOW to spend your time each day, week, or month. If you don't have a plan or know EXACTLY what to do, reach

out and get a coach who can help you with this FIRST!

10. **Embrace the right technology, team and systems** to support you so you can have more freedom!

When you put more of these things into action, you'll become more productive and that will allow you to:

1. Gain more hours back in your day.
2. Reach and impact many more people and prospects.
3. Sell more and make more money regularly.
4. Become more known and elevate your expert status.
5. Get more exposure and visibility.
6. If something tragic happens in your life, you will have the time and ability to handle it.

No one thinks anything tragic will happen to them of course, but I'd like to have you please rethink that. If I was talking to you right now in person, I would tell you my story and why it's made me so passionate about helping other entrepreneurs embrace and implement more systems and structure into their business. What I can tell you is that things were going along great about ten years into my business. In fact, I had just met the man of my dreams.

But within two years, I had to have two total hip replacement surgeries (at age 42 and 43) and my fiancé had kidney stones; then right after he proposed, he was diagnosed with throat cancer. Then a year later, my mom's husband died and I had to go help her out. A couple of years after that, she started falling at home and I had to fly to go help her again. She finally agreed to move closer to us so then we had to move her and sell her home and belongings. I could go on and on and on here, but I think you get what I'm trying to say is "life happens".

I could never have anticipated any of this happening but they did. All of them also took us out of our work or business for a minimum of a week if not a lot longer in the case of my surgeries.

I call this the "What If". What if something were to happen to you or a loved one? Would you make money if you couldn't work for a week or longer? If not, then you must, must, must set up appropriate systems, technology and team now so you're prepared just in case.

Don't avoid this or put it off. Ask for help or invest in resources and build yourself a successful, profitable business you love now!

For a few key free or low-cost trainings on how to do all of this or to have a conversation with me to see how I can help, please go to my website at www.JumpstartYourBizNow.com/freetrainings

or the main Trainings page where you'll find low-cost ways to learn how to delegate, what technology is right for your business, plus pricing strategies and more!

About the Author

Katrina Sawa

The JumpStart Your Biz Coach, Katrina Sawa, is the creator of the JumpStart Your Marketing & Sales Systems, and an Int'l Best-Selling author including *Love Yourself Successful* and *Jumpstart Your New Business Now*. She is the CEO of JumpstartYourBizNow.com and JumpstartPublishing.net. Katrina's no-nonsense approach develops consistently profitable businesses implementing proven marketing and business strategies. She's been featured on the Oprah and Friends XMRadioNetwork, ABC, TheCW and dozens of influential podcasts.

Jumpstart Your Side Hustle

Tips for Being a Successful, Well-Balanced, Mompreneur

By Denise Steele

Are you a mom or soon-to-be mom and know you want to have some sort of income coming in during your pregnancy and/or beyond?

Or are you someone who already has a family perhaps and needs more time with ADULTS? I get it!

Growing your family is an exciting and nervous occasion in itself, but what about when you also own a business or want to run a business?

I'm Denise and about six and a half years ago, I started my business selling home fragrances with a direct sales company. I loved the products so much that I wanted to get a better deal on what I was buying... sort of a cashback type of deal if you would.

Then it turned into more than that because so many people I spoke to also loved the products and I found myself being an entrepreneur! I later even got a business license and became official!

When I started having kids, however, my whole life changed dramatically. Has that sort of thing happened to you?

I have essentially changed how I run my business twice now because I am the mother of a four-year-old and a two-year-old. Being able to adapt how you run your business is the key to making the transition as seamless as possible from business owner to mompreneur. I am going to share with you some things that I have found beneficial and I hope that they will help you as well.

What to do before the baby arrives

- **Do** frontload your pregnancy with everything that you can. What is frontloading? I am talking about getting to as many meetings, hosting as many product parties, and getting out there as much as possible before the end of your third trimester.

- **Don't** frontload too early! Morning sickness can be rough and you don't want to have to cancel things if you have a regular first trimester morning sickness scenario.

- **Do** discuss with your child care person (if it isn't a child care center), how much they feel they can handle and to make sure that they let you know if they are being worn down.

- **Do** listen to your body. You don't want to be worn down from meetings and then find yourself tired and in labor.

I did fantastic at front-loading my second pregnancy and was going to keep networking and attending meetings up until a month before the due date, but my body was telling me otherwise. I felt that I had been very productive. So, I took the last two months off and went on my maternity leave from meetings early. Everyone completely understood.

Use the bump to help you stand out

Use your pregnancy to help you stand out and connect with others. Involve people in the journey that you really have no control over. I mean, the baby and your body decide how big you get, so just go along for the ride. I actually found this out after my pregnancy. People would come up to me and say, "Hey, you were the really pregnant lady who sold (my product) and would be at the luncheons, right?" Yep, that was me. I became known as the very, very pregnant-looking person who sold "blank". But guess what?! They remembered me and what did it cost me? Back pain and false labor? I'll take it. Over a year later, I still have people come up to me and say that even though they haven't been to a meeting in a while, they remember me because I showed up looking like I was about to burst.

Involve customers and prospective customers in the journey

- **Do** let your clients know you have a baby coming. People seem to love pregnancy announcements and games. Use that to your advantage! I ran many baby-related games on my Facebook business page and got new customers because of them. Grow your followers and promote your business without seemingly promoting your business. This will also give your clients a heads up that you may be slower to respond around delivery day and for a few weeks after.

- **Do** make gifts for the hospital/birthing staff. That last trimester is both the slowest and fastest trimester and if you aren't ready, you won't have time to get anything together. There are two reasons to give gifts to your hospital staff. One, they work hard and probably don't get treats or the full recognition they deserve. Two, if you make them feel special, I feel that it can help make everything more enjoyable for everyone. You have to plan your gifts out early. You can't be making little gift bags while in labor; that doesn't work. If possible, use your own products that you sell. Of course, make sure to label the items with your information or include a business card. If you don't have products to give, use individually wrapped cookies or some things that are sealed with your business card sticker.

Five things to remember

1. Some days you will get more done in your business than others

2. You started a side hustle so that you could put family first

3. Sometimes your needs (to-do list) go first so that you can be fully present with your child(ren)

4. Ask for help from family to watch them for a few hours so you can get work done

5. Find ways to involve them; if you can't do that, give them warnings that in a few minutes, it is mommy work time.

Networking and kids

- **Do** follow up.

- Remember that frontloading I talked about? I assume you would have gathered business cards and made connections with all of those people that you met at those networking meetings, right? Email them! It can be something as simple as saying that you will miss them at the next meeting because you just had your baby and you can share a picture and some information such as the baby's name. I suggest adding in that you would still like to help grow their business by referring people to them and that you are still working your business even with the new baby. You can even add that if they are referring anyone to you, to please let them know it may take a little longer for you to reply because of the new baby, but you will get back to them as quickly as possible.

- **Do** utilize your resources.

- I wanted to let everyone know that I didn't disappear and announce the newest assistant to my business, so I even paid to have an announcement with a picture added to our weekly member newsletter.

- **Do** contact the coordinator.

- Some groups will not allow kids, some will, or some don't share their opinion openly. This leads me to another reason to frontload your pregnancy: they already know you. They know you are involved and they know you work it. Ask the coordinator! Be open and see what can be done. I have found that some coordinators will allow infants that aren't mobile, some make a special meeting that you can attend, and some will even allow "just you" to bring your child because they trust you to use your judgement if the child becomes disruptive. With my second daughter, I was actually asked to bring her to my Chamber's luncheon because everyone wanted to see the baby that had been cooking for so long and to get their baby fix in. I then started a trend with other mom bosses bringing their small babies with them. As long as you use your judgement, I have found that most coordinators don't mind as long as no disruption is taking place.

- **Don't** bring the child(ren) if you don't have to. I will say, you get a lot less out of a meeting with an older baby in tow. I found myself focusing more on if she was staying quiet enough and so on that I was not able to focus on the educational training being provided.

Final tips

You, in the end, will find out what works for you. Perhaps your business can be run successfully during nap times or nursing times, or perhaps you need to block it in your schedule. I have had people come over just so that I can work while they play with the girls. I also put my office down in the playroom and have it separated with a baby gate. They can then play, I can still interact and play with them, but I can also work. Keep in mind, you may need to adjust some things as they get older.

Follow these steps, and you, too, can be a mompreneur like me! I want you to succeed as I have. **I have a great list of my favorite apps to help maximize work time while taking care of the children. If you want it, go to my site www.DeniseMompreneur.com and fill out my request form and I'll send it to you.**

About the Author
Denise Steele

Denise lives in Washington with her husband and her two children. Her business has earned many local awards, such as Chamber Member of the Year. Denise loves helping fellow small business owners grow their businesses. She loves coaching her team and has earned many training awards. Denise has a huge interest in history, and almost got a degree in Cultural Anthropology instead of her degrees in Early Childhood Education.

Jumpstart Your Website

The Keys to Making It the HUB of Your Business

By Lori Osborne

I am writing this in 2021, approximately 18 months into the COVID pandemic, and we are definitely seeing changes in how businesses operate, most moving more of their sales to online. In fact, according to Digital Commerce 360, e-commerce grew 44% in 2020 over the previous year. Though this was done out of necessity, many of these businesses are now seeing how profitable online sales can be. Look at Amazon as an example! Unfortunately, however, not every small business is experiencing success online. Why is that?

There are 2 things it takes to be successful online:

1. A solid digital marketing strategy
2. A website that effectively incorporates your digital marketing strategy

Frankly, your business can have the best product or service there is to offer and for the very best price, but if your potential customers don't even know the product or service exists, it doesn't matter. And in the digitally driven world we are in today, where people are distracted in an instant by a tweet, text, or TikTok post, it is more critical than ever that small businesses reach your prospects in the digital world.

Your website is the hub of your digital presence so it must effectively do the job of attracting potential clients, engaging those prospects in what you have to offer, and ultimately moving the prospects through the sales funnel.

Before we look at the details specific to websites, let's discuss why you even need a website for your business. You may believe that you can run your business through social media since there are so many options available today, but social media is only one spoke in the digital marketing wheel, and it is definitely not robust enough to be the hub for digitally marketing your business. You may also wonder if you need a website if you're not selling anything online. The answer is still yes. You may not be selling your products and services online – you may not even BE online – but your customers are! Remember, over half of the world and 85% of the US are on the Internet, and most of them go to the Internet (specifically Google) to find what they are looking for.

The first thing to decide when looking at developing a website, or updating one, is whether to use a professional or do it yourself. There are several factors to consider here:

- Your budget
- Your technical ability
- Your design ability
- Your understanding of marketing and how to best appeal to your potential clients
- The time and energy you have to dedicate to the process

The short answer here, though, is that you should absolutely invest in having a professional build your website. The templates generally look good and can be fairly easy to use, but they are not custom to your business, your brand, and what your prospects need to see and hear.

There are several things to consider when hiring a professional to build or update your website. First and foremost, do you connect with them and do you like their work? The connection between a web developer and business owner is crucial since the web developer needs to understand you, your brand, your market, and your business model in order to build a website that will attract and convert your prospects to clients. This connection also extends to the style and approach. If you find you do not like the design style of the website developer, there's a high probability that you also will not connect with them on the proper approach for your project.

Some other factors to consider when evaluating professionals are:

- What platform do they use? Is it something you can support yourself if you want to?

- How much marketing knowledge and experience do they have?

- How is their reputation? Were they referred to you? How are their online reviews?

- What are their quality control and revisions processes? Do they limit the number of changes you can make in the initial design? Do they guarantee your satisfaction with the website? These are all hints at their integrity and how they do business.

- What do they charge? Is it market value? If it is underpriced, you will probably not get the quality you need, especially in the marketing piece. If it is over-priced, what are you getting for the extra investment?

Once you have decided on who you are going to use to develop your website, it's time to start planning the content. Yes, some of this will come from the developer who should have the marketing savvy to guide you, but there are still key elements that can only come from you.

The first thing that needs a clear definition is your customer avatar (be specific as possible here). What are they attracted to visually? What words and phrases do they use?

Secondly, you need to choose your URL/domain name and create your business logo.

The next thing you need to do is plan the pages and functionality you want for the website as there are a lot of options. Of course, you will have a Home page, a Contact page, and typically an About page, but have you thought about your Call to Action (CTA)? This is the most important item for any website. Remember, your new website visitor has likely never met you and is on your website to investigate and learn about your business. Unless you are running a pure e-commerce site, they are probably not here to make a major purchase. Consider this when determining your CTA. You want to move new prospects through the sales funnel, not push for a big sale. This is much like the first date in a relationship. You don't ask someone to marry you on the first date when you are still determining if you even have a connection with them. Therefore, your CTA (for a non-e-commerce business) should encourage an easy yes like signing up for a freebie in exchange for their email address. (In contrast, an e-commerce site will have "Buy Now" as the CTA.)

And that leads us to the next most important thing for your website...your freebie. The freebie is just that, something that would be valuable to your customer avatar, but costs them nothing. This can be a downloadable guide, valuable tips, a short video training, a short coaching video, or even a free trial of a program or membership you offer. The key is that it is something OF VALUE to your avatar, valuable enough to encourage them to provide their email in exchange. In other words, five tips that everyone on the planet knows would not be valuable, but five tips that could save them significant time or money or a free eBook that provides information that could directly impact their life or business are of value to your audience.

It is important to point out here that offering a free 15-minute or even 30-minute call is not a valuable freebie to most prospects. If someone meets you or hears about you and they are specifically looking to contact you, having a clear link on the Home page to schedule these calls is important, but do not confuse this with a freebie. The vast majority of prospects will consider this a sales call no matter what you name it; therefore, they will not consider that a valuable freebie so you will likely lose their attention when they visit your website.

Now that we have the most important functions of the website covered, where you really want to focus is outlining your pages. In a detailed eBook that I created for you, I outlined all kinds of possible pages that I didn't have room to share in this chapter.

Finally, making sure your website is seen as high as possible on Google and has adequate SEO (Search Engine

Optimization) on every page and post is essential to finish off the site.

Are you ready to take your marketing to the next level through a website that WORKS?

An exceptional website is so much more than a bunch of pictures thrown into a template. Your website is the HUB of your business and should be designed with that in mind. Yes, your website should look good, but, even more importantly, it should attract prospects and should facilitate converting those prospects into paying clients!

That's where I come in...
I specialize in building websites that WORK for small businesses, solopreneurs, and non-profit organizations... for people like you who are smart and talented but don't have the time, energy, and/or technical and marketing expertise to build and maintain the website that truly is the hub of your organization.

If you are looking for help:

I would be guilty of "do as I say and not as I do" if I did not offer you some sort of freebie, right? No worries. Of course, I did! **Go to www.bizbolster.com/jumpstart for the following freebies:**

- The extended version of this chapter in a Jumpstart Your Website eBook which includes a long list of the types of webpages you could want on your website

- An SEO checklist

- Instructions for setting up your Google My Business account and Google Analytics

- Logo design tips and resources

- Tips on how to create your Digital Marketing Strategy and more

Here's to achieving successful online marketing for your business!

About the Author

Lori Osborne

Lori is the Founder and Chief Solution Architect for BizBolster Web Solutions. She specializes in digital marketing for small businesses, including custom website development, reputation management, sales funnels, and SEO services. Lori has 30+ years' small business and Information Technology experience and has been a business owner for 15+ years. She is married to the love of her life, and they live in Florida with their two wonderful fur babies.

What's Next?

What did you think of the stories and expertise that our authors had to share?

Did you learn a few new things to take back to your life or work?

My hope is that you did learn a few things, or at least walk away with a fresh new way of thinking about some of our topics. If so, please go over to Amazon and leave us a review! Make sure you choose the "green" colored *Jumpstart Your* _____ book as there are three others there.

Our authors have been hand-selected due to their level of expertise, genuine integrity, and overall skill level in their industry. If you enjoyed reading some of their stories or learning more about how they help their clients, please take the next step and reach out to those who spoke to you.

Most of the authors in this book speak to groups of all sizes, both in person and virtually. They also offer products, programs, events, and services that can support you in one or more areas of your life, health, or business / career.

I highly recommend that you take advantage of their special offers, additional downloads, and more when you visit each of the websites listed at the end of their chapters.

In addition, I've put together ONE page on my website where you can access all of the Jumpstart Author's websites and special offers, to make it easy for you to follow up. **Go to www.JumpstartBookAuthors.com** right now, before you forget who you wanted to connect with or find out more about. All authors from all Jumpstart books are on that page.

Thank you for reading this book, and I look forward to bringing you more Jumpstart Your _____ Authors in upcoming books, plus more training and teachings in my own books.

If you are an author who has something that YOU help people JUMPSTART and you would like to be considered as one of our next Jumpstart Authors, please go to www.BecomeAJumpstartAuthor.com now and apply!

WHAT DO YOU HELP YOUR CLIENTS JUMPSTART?

In the *Jumpstart Your _____* book series, YOU Fill in the Blank with the thing YOU do with YOUR clients for YOUR chapter, and become an author this year! Use this book as a MARKETING TOOL to get leads and grow your business.

Interested in becoming an author easily?

Get into a compilation book of 12-20 authors and write ONE chapter, but get huge exposure for you and your business, along with every author promoting it alongside you! Attract new clients and make more money after your prospects are introduced to you in this book.

Want to get more exposure, speaking gigs, or clients in the coming year? Become an author!

While it could take a while for you to write your own full book, it's relatively easy to get published in an anthology or compilation book by just writing one chapter. Everyone in the book promotes the books and sells them, so you get in front of a lot more people than you would with just your own book. PLUS... we do all the work! **Find out how this could benefit you here:**

www.BecomeAJumpstartAuthor.com

ABOUT KATRINA SAWA

CEO OF K. SAWA MARKETING INT'L INC.
AND JUMPSTART PUBLISHING

Katrina Sawa is known as the JumpStart Your Biz Coach because she literally kicks her clients and their businesses into high gear, online & offline, and fast. Katrina is the creator of the JumpStart Your Marketing® System, JumpStart Your Business System, Jumpstart Yourself as a Speaker System. She is an International Best-Selling Author with 16 books and CEO of Jumpstart Publishing as well. Katrina's first, hosted anthology book, *Jumpstart Your* _____ was published in Fall of 2018 and now every year Kat gets to help 12-20 entrepreneurs become authors as a new volume of *Jumpstart Your* _____ is published annually.

Katrina helps entrepreneurs make smarter marketing and business decisions in order to create the life and business of your dreams. She helps you create your big picture vision, plan and initial offerings if you're just starting out. She helps you develop a more leveraged, efficient business and marketing plan if you're more seasoned. Either way, she shows you all the steps, systems and marketing that need to be put in place in order to accomplish your big picture business, life and money goals. She does this via one-on-one coaching, her Live Big Mastermind, her Jumpstart Events, Webinars, Podcasts, and numerous Facebook groups she runs.

Katrina is the CEO of the International Speaker Network that meets twice monthly on Zoom for networking, resources and collaboration. She won the National Collaborator of the Year Award by the Public Speakers Association of who's conference which Katrina spoke for four years in a row. She is also a member of the Women's Speaker Association, eWomenNetwork, Women's Prosperity Network and a Diamond Member of Polka Dot Powerhouse. Kat speaks to groups and conferences of all sizes all over North America and the Internet.

One thing that makes Katrina different is that she also focuses on her clients' personal lives. She found that most business owners lack enough self-confidence to truly enable them to get to their next level, or take those leaps of faith they need to achieve their ultimate dreams. Katrina's goal is to inspire, motivate, and educate entrepreneurs on how to love themselves fully, live a bigger life, and leverage themselves to complete happiness.

Katrina has a degree in Business Administration, Marketing Concentration, from California State University Sacramento, and has been a featured business expert on three of her local television news channels throughout her career thus far. She has also been featured in the Los Angeles Tribune, Comstock's Magazine, Lead Up for Women Magazine, Top Talent Magazine, and Amazing Women Magazine.

Katrina lives in Northern California with her husband Jason, step-daughter Riley, and their German Shepherd, Willow.

You can find out all about Kat and her products, programs, services, and live events online at
www.JumpstartYourBizNow.com
and
www.JumpstartPublishing.net.

Motivate and Inspire Others!
"Share this Book"

Retail $16.95 + Tax & Shipping

Special Quantity Discounts

5 - 15 Books	$11.95 Each
16 - 30 Books	$9.95 Each
30 - 1,000 Books	$7.95 Each

To Place an Order Contact:

K. Sawa Marketing International Inc.
916-872-4000

info@JumpstartYourBizNow.com

or go to www.JumpstartPublishing.net

Grab One or More of the Jumpstart Your Business Free Trainings Now!

Learn How to:

- Get Started Speaking
- Jumpstart Your Business
- Implement Best Marketing Practices
- Build an Effective
- Website
- Create a Life You Love
- Find Your Purpose
- Love Yourself Successful
- Delegate & Build Your Team
- And more!

Get Access Online at:

www.JumpstartYourBizNow.com/FreeTrainings

Want a Deeper Training on How to Start, Grow, Market & Monetize Your Business?

- In Depth Training, How-To, Templates
- Roadmap & Plan to Jumpstart Your Biz
- Hot Seat Coaching
- Learn from Topic Specific Speakers
- Mastermind & Network
- Make Money with Easy YES Offers

Attend One of Kat's Live Events! Get Information at www.JumpstartEvents.net

Book Katrina to Speak:

K. Sawa Marketing International Inc.
PO Box 6, Roseville, CA 95661
916-872-4000 | info@JumpstartYourBizNow.com
www.JumpstartYourBizNow.com/speaking

Made in the USA
Monee, IL
28 November 2021

83253577R00095